The 'Net, the Web, and You

All You Really Need to Know About the Internet ... And a Little Bit More

Daniel J. Kurland

 Wadsworth Publishing Company

I(T)P® An International Thomson Publishing Company

Belmont • Albany • Bonn • Boston • Cincinnati • Detroit • London
Madrid • Melbourne • Mexico City • New York • Paris • San Francisco
Singapore • Tokyo • Toronto • Washington

T5-AFS-517

Editor: Angela Gantner Wrahtz
Editorial Assistant: Royden Tonomura
Production Editor: Jennie Redwitz
Designer: Andrew H. Ogus
Print Buyer: Barbara Britton
Permissions Editor: Bob Kauser
Art Editor/Illustrator: Beth Okurowski
Copy Editor: Jean Schiffman
Cover: Andrew H. Ogus
Compositor: Margarite Reynolds
Cover/Art Assistance: Carole Lawson, Craig Hanson
Printer: Malloy Lithographing, Inc.

COPYRIGHT © 1996 by Wadsworth Publishing Company
A Division of International Thomson Publishing Inc.
I(T)P The ITP logo is a registered trademark under license.

Printed in the United States of America
1 2 3 4 5 6 7 8 9 10

For more information, contact Wadsworth Publishing Company.

Wadsworth Publishing Company
10 Davis Drive
Belmont, California 94002, USA

International Thomson Editores
Campos Eliseos 385, Piso 7
Col. Polanco
11560 México D.F. México

International Thomson Publishing Europe
Berkshire House 168-173
High Holborn
London, WC1V 7AA, England

International Thomson Publishing GmbH
Königswinterer Strasse 418
53227 Bonn, Germany

Thomas Nelson Australia
102 Dodds Street
South Melbourne 3205
Victoria, Australia

International Thomson Publishing Asia
221 Henderson Road
#05-10 Henderson Building
Singapore 0315

Nelson Canada
1120 Birchmount Road
Scarborough, Ontario
Canada M1K 5G4

International Thomson Publishing Japan
Hirakawacho Kyowa Building, 3F
2-2-1 Hirakawacho
Chiyoda-ku, Tokyo 102, Japan

Library of Congress Cataloging-in-Publication Data
Kurland, Daniel, J.
    The 'Net, the Web, and you : all you really need to know about the Internet...
and a little bit more / Daniel J. Kurland.
        p.   cm.
    ISBN 0-534-51281-X (pbk.)
    1. Internet (Computer network) 2. World Wide Web (information retrieval
system) I. Title
TK5105.875.I57K87   1996
004.6'7–dc20   95-43656

Contents

I   Background and Perspective 1

1   Introduction 3

An Abundance of Information 4
Finding Out What's There and Where It Is 7
Figuring Out How to Get What You Want 8

2   Telecommunications: From the Flintstones to the Fax 9

Speech 10
Writing 11
Mail Service 12
Printing 12
The Telegraph and Telecommunications 13
The Telephone 13
Wireless Communication 14
Electronic Storage 14
Storing Sound 14
The Computer Age 15
Electronic Images 16

**3   Bulletin Boards, On-line Services,
and the Birth of the Internet 17**

The Modem 19
Bulletin Boards 19

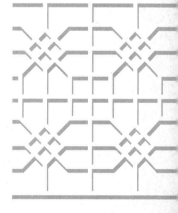

On-line Services 22
ARPAnet, NSFnet, and Packet Switching 25
The Internet 27

II The Internet 33

4 Some Internet Basics 35

Internet Providers 36
Internet Addresses 36
The Command Prompt 38
Uniform Resource Locators (URLs) 38

5 Telnet: The Internet as Remote Control 41

Overview 42
Using Telnet 43
Internet Services 44

6 Electronic Mail (E-mail): The Internet as Post Office 47

Overview 48
Using E-mail 51
Text Versus Graphic E-mail Programs 52
Social Aspects of E-mail 52

7 Mailing Lists, Newsgroups, Talk and Chat: The Internet as Bulletin Board, Bull Session, and Party Line 55

Mailing Lists: An Overview 56
Using Mailing Lists 58
Discussion Groups: An Overview 58
Using Discussion Groups 59
Newsgroups: An Overview 63

Using Newsgroups 66
Newsgroups: Perspective 68
Talk and Chat Programs: An Overview 71
Using Talk and Chat Programs 71

8   File Transfer Protocol: The Internet as Lending Library 75

Introduction 76
Overview 77
Accessing FTP 78
Using FTP 79

9   Archie: The Card Catalog 85

Overview 86
Accessing Archie 87
Whatis? 90

10   Gopher: The Internet as Research Library 93

Overview 94
Accessing Gopher 97
An Example 100
Graphic-Interface Programs 104
FTP Versus Gopher 106

11   Veronica: Searching with Gopher 107

Overview 108
Accessing Veronica 109
Using Veronica 110
Text Versus Graphic Interface 112

12   WAIS: Searching Documents 115

Overview 116
Using WAIS 118
Some Concerns 123
Perspective 124

13 The World Wide Web: The Internet as Multimedia 125

   The Look! 128
   What's Behind It All: Hypertext 128
   Accessing the World Wide Web 132
   Using the World Wide Web 132
   The Glory and the Hype 133

III Doing Research on the Internet 139

14 General Concerns 141

   Research Is Initiated by Questions 142
   Research Is Guided by Knowledge and Reflection 143
   Research Is Driven by Feedback 144
   Other Factors 144

15 Internet Concerns 145

   Try the Obvious First 146
   Selecting Internet Resources 147
   Networking for Knowledge 147
   Order and Organization 148
   Assumptions of Authenticity 149
   Budgeting Time 150
   Citations and Plagiarism 150

16 Internet Resources for Research 153

   Desk Reference Tools 155
   Subject Guides 159
   Discipline-Specific Guides 160
   Key-Word Search Programs 162
   Finding Search Programs 166
   Tactics and Strategies 168

IV Issues 171

17 Controversy, Concerns, and Future Developments 173

The First Amendment, Personal Rights,
Public Taste, and Censorship 174

Anonymity, License, and Security 176

Privatization and Commercialization 178

Other Inherent Problems and Concerns 180

Appendices 183

A Some Computer Basics 185

Text Versus Graphic Displays 186

Commands Versus Point and Click 186

Unix 187

Shareware and Commercial Software 187

Files 189

Viruses 190

Directories and Subdirectories 190

Computing Versus Housekeeping 191

Choices and Limits 191

File Storage Formats 192

Encoding Files 193

Archiving Files 194

Compressing Files 194

B Getting on the Internet 197

The Options 198

On-line Services 199

Shell Accounts 200

SLIP/PPP 200

Network Access 201

Recommendations 202

Glossary 203

Preface

The Internet. Everyone's talking about it. Which is probably why you are looking at this book in the first place. But there are more important reasons for understanding the Internet.

The Internet provides an opportunity to expand not only your knowledge but your perspective. It is at once a mailbox, a research tool, a vehicle of commerce, and a medium of entertainment.

You can send a letter to a colleague in Japan, locate a grant announcement, check the score of the last Bullets game and the progress of a Senate bill, order a present for Aunt Harriet's birthday, listen to a sample track from a new CD, and find a recipe using avocados for supper tonight.

More to the point, the Internet offers access to an international community of ideas. If information is power, the Internet can arm us all.

WHO THIS BOOK IS FOR

This book assumes no particular computer knowledge or expertise. It is intended for everyone who, however reluctantly, has decided it's finally time to understand what everyone else is talking about.

It is intended for students, for researchers, and for administrators and their staffs. It is intended for all who will seek, or are now seeking, employment in an increasingly computer-based marketplace. It is intended for those who own a computer, use one at work, or have never used one. And it is designed for everyone with access to the Internet who uses it only for E-mail.

The Overall Approach: A General Understanding

There are many ways to access the Internet and many programs for browsing the Internet. You can gain access from home, an office network, or a university-wide network. Your computer may use Microsoft Windows, DOS, or Macintosh System 7. How you access the Internet will vary, but the general principles remain the same.

Once on the Internet, you can search for information in a variety of ways. You can browse a series of menus, use search programs, or follow ideas from one document to another. You can search by topic, by term, or by file name. You can browse the World Wide Web with a program called Mosaic, or with Netscape, or with Cello. Here again, the need for a broad understanding is apparent.

Our primary concern then is not to offer lists of commands and Internet addresses–although we will do that for those who want them. The main goal is to provide an overall understanding that will enable you to use any and all programs efficiently. The aim is to empower present and future users.

What This Book Offers

This book is ultimately a primer on the Internet. It explains what the Internet offers and how the tools for accessing that information work.

It maintains a simple narrative throughout, explaining the basic principles, concepts, and concerns. In addition, it offers lists of basic commands and resources, as well as anecdotes and trivia that provide a flavor of Internet culture.

Throughout, an effort has been made to simplify but not to "dumb down." While geek-talk and smileys are part of the vernacular of the Internet, and are explained here, every effort is made to speak in plain English, to say "connect to a remote computer" rather than "telnet to a host."

How This Book Is Organized

The 'Net, the Web, and You is in essence a number of books in one.

Part One offers an overview of the origins of the Internet. It places the Internet within the broader historical development of human communication, from the printed word to electronic bulletin boards and on-line services.

Part Two provides an introduction to the services of the Internet–what they are, what they offer, and how to use them. The discussion includes illustrations of text-based systems to indicate the basic commands and, with that, the underlying operations. Illustrations of graphic-interface systems suggest the convenience of the latest programs.

Part Three examines tactics and techniques for doing research, both in general and on the Internet in particular. This section includes listings of major resources.

Part Four explores social, political, and economic issues confronting the growth and development of the Internet in the coming years.

Appendix A covers an introduction to key concepts of computer use for readers unfamiliar with computers operations. Other readers can draw on this section for reference on topics such as archiving and encoding. Appendix B discusses the various ways to get on the Internet. The book ends with a Glossary.

Ultimately, the best way to discover the Internet is on the Internet. This book is designed to get you started and to be your companion as you explore.

ACKNOWLEDGMENTS

I wish to thank the following reviewers for their helpful suggestions in the early stages of this project: Donald R. Cloud, Virginia Polytechnic Institute; Alan Fried, University of South Carolina; Bill Osher, Georgia Institute of Technology; Lauren Pernetti, Kent State University; and Robert S. Staley, Colorado Technical College.

I am indebted to Luther Keeler of moontower.com for his ever generous help as I first encountered the Internet; to my editor, Angela Gantner Wrahtz, for her enthusiasm for my efforts; and to my wife, Gail, whose gift of a new modem started this project and whose gift of support and encouragement made it possible.

Background and Perspective

1

Introduction

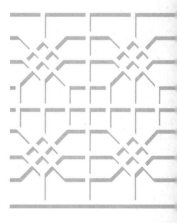

In articles and discussion, commentators portray the Internet with a variety of images. They make allusions to road systems ("the electronic superhighway"), "Star Trek" adventurers ("internauts in cyberspace"), and to a world community (the "electronic global village"). Encountering the Internet has been compared to discovering the Library of Congress, the Louvre, Disneyland, and a Sears catalog for the first time or to suddenly confronting short-wave radio or five-hundred-channel cable television.

AN ABUNDANCE OF INFORMATION

Internet enthusiasts often attempt to entice the uninitiated with lists of resources. They start with large general classifications:

- Academic and public library catalogs
- Electronic texts (Shakespeare, Mark Twain, *Alice in Wonderland,* and so forth)
- Encyclopedias and dictionaries
- Interactive games
- Business and financial information
- Discussion groups
- Government documents and statistics

They continue with more specific and intriguing examples:

- Stadium and arena seating charts
- The Martha's Vineyard ferry schedule
- Pictures of the galaxy from the Hubble spacecraft

- A searchable database of song lyrics
- A digitalized atlas of the human body based on actual photographs of cross sections of a corpse

The resources of the Internet are indeed enormous and are ever expanding. Resources unheard of only a few years ago are now commonplace.

If you engage in any form of research, for profit or pleasure, whether as lawyer, student, citizen or traveler, cattle farmer or football fan, the Internet can prove a useful tool. If you are intrigued by contemporary culture, are energized by frank discussion of current political topics, or simply delight in discovering the resources of the latest in multimedia entertainment, the Internet has something for you.

One way to suggest the resources of the Internet is through the Internet Hunt. In September 1992, Rick Gates, a student and lecturer at the University of Arizona, created a monthly Internet scavenger hunt to test users' knowledge and resourcefulness. Many of the questions are of his own making; others are sent in by readers. Answers are mailed to Gates, who posts correct answers at various sites within a week or so after each hunt has ended. The hunt is now administered by a team of volunteers and focuses on the resources of the World Wide Web.

The following, for June 1994, is a special hunt for first-timers.*

THE INTERNET HUNT
QUESTIONS
for June, 1994
entries due by midnight, June 11 (-0700)
Total Points: 28

Question 1 (3 points)

This summer I'd like to go white-water rafting with some friends. I need to get some gear—what information can I get about white-water outfitters on the Internet?

Question 2 (3 points)

I have just started to use the Internet and notice that people use lots of funny symbols at the end of their sentences. Someone told me these are smileys. Is there a list of them on the net somewhere?

*Reprinted by permission of the Internet Hunt Team.

Question 3 (3 points)

How can I find out what the requirements are for U.S. citizens traveling to Belize?

Question 4 (2 points)

What two statewide (North Carolina) educational telecommunication services (Bulletin Boards) are reachable via a gopher menu (as well as a telnet command)?

HINT: Which freenet did you use to locate them?

Question 5 (3 points)

My child was given a storywriting assignment in which she must use animals from *Alice's Adventures in Wonderland* as characters in her work. I've heard I can find an ASCII (text) version of Lewis Carroll's story somewhere on the Internet, but I don't know where to begin. Please tell me where I can find it and list six animals from the story.

Question 6 (3 points)

What is the name of the exhibit that will be at the California Museum of Photography between Sept. 10 and Nov. 20, 1994?

Question 7 (3 points)

We are studying French history in my high school French IV class. Our instructor said there were two novels available on the Net that would help our understanding of two periods in particular, the French Revolution of 1793 and the later French Revolution of 1830. I can't remember the names of these novels for the life of me, but I believe he said Charles Dickens wrote one of them and Victor Hugo wrote the other one. Can you tell me the names of these novels and where on the Internet can I find them?

Question 8 (3 points)

A teacher at my daughter's school developed this fascinating "Wolf Study" unit for her third-grade pupils. She said that she found much of the information at a Gopher site on the Internet. She downloaded telemetry data, study guides, behavioral data, photo-quality images, wolf howls, and even the utilities to convert the images and sounds–all in one place! Where is this Gopher and how can I find it?

Question 9 (2 points)

I've been moving around the Internet for a few months now, and a couple of terms keep popping up that I'm not familiar with. The first term is URL and it's usually followed by a long line that looks like it contains some sort of access information. The second term, *http,* often shows up at the beginning of that long line. Could you tell me what URL and *http* stand for?

Question 10 (3 points)

OK, I think I'm getting it now. World Wide Web is sort of like Gopher, but it's based on hypertext. As with Gopher, one can access "Web" servers all over the world. The trouble is, on the system I connect to, I can run telnet and Gopher, but there doesn't seem to be any local software for a Web client to talk to all those servers. Can you give me the address of three World Wide Web clients that I can telnet to and use?

Extra Credit (1 point)

Where is the final match of the 1994 World Cup being held?

Mystery Question

Has anybody found a picture of that galaxy-gobbling black hole that the Hubble space telescope recently discovered?

Finding Out What's There and Where It Is

To find answers on the Internet to specific questions, you must have some idea of what's out there and know how to find what you want when you want it. As the Internet Hunt suggests, finding information on the Internet can be challenging, even daunting.

Discovering the resources of the Internet is much like finding out what is on cable television. Instead of learning times and channels, you learn Internet addresses. The comparison between television and the Internet can be carried only so far, however. Unlike television, the Internet is constantly increasing in size and complexity. Anything you find will probably still be there the next day or a month later–although maybe at a new address. You can never truly know all that's out there, let alone experience it.

Source: Geoff Olson. Reprinted by permission.

FIGURING OUT HOW TO GET WHAT YOU WANT

Knowing what is on the Internet, and where it is, is only half the battle. You also have to know how to get where you want to go. You must understand a variety of services (such as Gophers and the World Wide Web) and the programs necessary to access those services. Also, to use the services effectively, you must understand how each service organizes and stores information.

Finally, to use the Internet–and your own time–effectively, you must distinguish between active discovery and idle diversion, between productive research and sheer busywork. As with any tool, you must figure out how to use the Internet efficiently for your own purposes.

While the Internet may have the richness and range of a world-class encyclopedia, this does not mean you want or need to read every article. Just because you can download thousands of files does not mean you need any of them. Just because hundreds of people wrote in to the newsgroup *alt.alien.visitors!* does not mean you are obligated to read what they said. While you might be interested in a World Wide Web site devoted to movies (*http://www.msstate.edu/Movies**), you probably have little need to spend time visiting the Barbie doll on the Internet (OK, if you must: *http://deeptht.armory.com/~zenugirl/ barbie.html*).

---

*For an explanation of Internet addresses such as this, see the discussion of Uniform Resource Locators (URLs) in Chapter 4.

> Nobody has ever dropped off the network. Once they get on, they get hooked. It's like selling drugs.
> Dan Van Belleghem, National Science Foundation

2

Telecommunications

From the Flintstones to the Fax

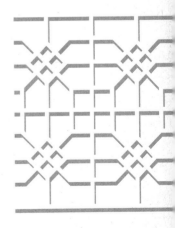

Introduction - Internet

Many of the picturesque images used to describe the Internet in the previous chapter are evocative–but they are only partially useful. By stressing notions of newness and uniqueness, we only confuse ourselves. In fact, the basic concepts of the Internet are hardly new. The Polaroid camera is more magical, the development of the telegraph more revolutionary.

The Internet is best viewed within the historical development of human communication. At heart, it is merely a new stage in humankind's ongoing attempt to meet people, exchange information, and explore the world of ideas.

We begin then with a discussion–sometimes fanciful and obviously superficial–of human communication. The goal is not to offer a comprehensive history but to review concepts essential to understanding the Internet.

As you read, let your mind seesaw between the past and the present, between early inventions and recent technology. Note how each new step mirrors earlier advances; the technology just gets faster, more efficient, and covers a wider area than before.

SPEECH

In the beginning was the word. People spoke to one another, face to face. They asked questions, gave directions, expressed their feelings, exchanged ideas, and complained about the weather. They gossiped and shared information much as they do today on the Internet or elsewhere.

intents —

But, as they say, you had to be there—literally. All communication was local. You could only talk to someone in front of your nose or within shouting distance. While a few storytellers remembered mythological adventures, most people struggled to recall what they had for lunch. You couldn't "look something up"; the best you could do was ask someone and hope that person remembered. If no one remembered, for all intents and purposes, it didn't happen. History was the collective memory of the group.

Initially, language was essentially a unifying force. People were joined by their ability to share ideas. But communication required that people speak the same language; the distinction between friend and stranger, citizen and foreigner, was manifest in language. Going beyond the immediate cultural environment required translation or the universal language of gesture.

communication literally.

Struggle to recall what they did yesterday

language unifying force and distinction

cultural environment Need Translation

WRITING

How did writing began? forgetable

Like thoughts and dreams, speech is ephemeral. At first, people drew pictures to capture ideas and images. Later came symbols, then an alphabet. With writing, the recording of language, speech could in effect be stored. Information could be archived and retrieved; ideas could be distributed among a wider audience. And with writing, expertise—or claims to such—could be captured for all time.

by drawing pictures—ideas images and then symbols " alphabet " writing

> There is no longer any doubt that [computers] will reshape human civilization even more quickly and more thoroughly than did the printing press. Gutenberg's invention, which so empowered Jefferson and his colleagues in their fight for democracy, seems to pale before the rise of electronic communications and innovations, from the telegraph to television, to the microprocessor and the emergence of a new computerized world—the information age.
>
> Al Gore, "Infrastructure for the Global Village," *Scientific American*, September 1991, reprinted in *The Computer in the 21st Century*, Special Issue, *Scientific American*, 1995.

Reading in to a question

read mark

and antote each

Write some ideas of summary at the end

Various attempts at distant communication had been tried prior to writing, and even after: drums, semaphore, smoke signals, homing pigeons, and signal fires. Yet the ability to capture speech as writing was the first step toward enabling efficient communication across large distances.

Problems of translation still remained and social divisions were still fostered. Class barriers existed between those who could read and write and those who couldn't. "Illiterate" was soon no longer a description but an epithet. And the record was of course only partial. We learn about earlier civilizations not from the discussions of the common person but from the literature of the elite.

Mail Service

Early communication over a distance was based on riders and a network of relay stations. As populations and the postal systems expanded, reference to "the blacksmith in Boston" no longer sufficed. Messages had to be sorted and routed to increasingly precise addresses. An address such as "the blacksmith at the stable in the market in Boston" might do the job. (Years later, *blacksmith@stable.market.boston* might not seem so strange!)

Printing

The time and labor of reproducing handwritten manuscripts limited the audience, and with it the subject matter, of written texts. Then, in the mid-1440s, Johann Gutenberg perfected movable type—as well as transforming the wine press into a device for intellectual pursuits! Both the Koreans and Chinese had experimented with movable type during the 11th century, but Gutenberg had the advantage of a simpler alphabet.

Manual labor yielded to the machine. The price of books dropped and the number and variety increased. Ideas could be disseminated widely, at least by those who could afford to print their work. Printing combined with the mail system permitted subscriptions to published materials.

The invention of printing spawned the growth of libraries and of centralized research. Knowledge could be warehoused for later retrieval. Again, this was nothing new—only more efficient. As many as thirty thousand clay tablets had been stored in Nippur in ancient Mesopotamia and five hundred thousand papyrus scrolls at Alexandria, Egypt, before the Christian era.

THE TELEGRAPH AND TELECOMMUNICATIONS

Centuries passed. For the most part, distant communication remained slow and inefficient. Not until the harnessing of electricity less than two hundred years ago did telecommunication–instant communication beyond the range of sight or hearing–finally became a reality.

It began with the telegraph. Initially used for signaling purposes on British railroads, the telegraph became a tool for communication when Samuel Morse developed a code to associate short and long signals (dots and dashes) with the letters of the alphabet (Morse code). The history of telecommunications would then be a history of techniques for translating sounds and images into different forms of electronic signals for storage and transmission.

For centuries, the speed of complex communication had been limited by the fastest mode of land transportation, about twenty-five miles per hour. Now it was limited only by the speed of the telegrapher's hand. The signals were seemingly instantaneous. Cables soon stretched across the country and by 1858 across the Atlantic. A network of wires ran where a network of roads, sea lanes, or tracks had gone before.

THE TELEPHONE

Progress now came rapidly. In only a blink of the historical eye, Alexander Graham Bell figured out how to make electronic signals mirror the sound waves of human speech. As telephone service expanded, local telephone networks were linked to regional networks, which were joined with national and international networks.

The telephone would have major social, political, and economic impact on society and its institutions. Above all, it provided a direct person-to-person link, a mechanism of truly democratic communication–at least for those rich enough to afford one.

Once homes and offices were wired together by the telephone, the connecting cables could be put to other uses. The 1990s would see the flourishing of the fax (facsimile) machine to transmit images, utilizing a process police departments and newspapers had been using since the 1920s. (The process became more rapid, and thus commercially feasible, with the ability to digitize the image—to reduce it to a series of ones and zeros—not unlike the earlier dots and dashes of Morse code.)

WIRELESS COMMUNICATION

How does wireless communication work? radiation of sound energy

Throughout the 19th century, telecommunications consisted of communication by wire. At the turn of the century, "wireless" telegraph, and then radio, freed communication from that physical barrier. Radio radiated to everyone who tuned in, offering an efficient means of mass communications distinct from the person-to-person contact of the telephone.

ELECTRONIC STORAGE

How does Electronic Storage work? extend one's reach.

One normally thinks of advances in the *means* of communication as the truly revolutionary developments in human communication. Thus, the impact of the telephone is equated with that of the printing press.

An argument can be made, however, that having the means of *transmitting* sound across long distances, even instantaneously, only extends one's reach; it is equivalent to learning to yell louder but does not truly advance communication. True change, as with the inventions of writing and publishing, did not involve a *means* of communication so much as a means of *storing* communications. (In much the same way, the case can be made that the critical invention underlying photography was not the camera but the film plate in the 1850s.)

equivalent to learning to yell louder but not truly advanced communication.

STORING SOUND

How do we store sound?

The development of telecommunications mirrors advances in generating and storing sound. Soon after Bell first transmitted sound electronically, Thomas Edison invented a means to store and reproduce

offering an efficient means of mass communication instead of Person to Person.

Truely revolutionary developments

Bell — transmitted sound electronically

Thomas — means to store and reproduce sound.

sound: the phonograph—or, more accurately, the wax cylinder (storage) and the phonograph (reproduction). It was the former accomplishment that would actually usher in the computer age.

Sound can be stored in various forms. With the wax cylinders of Edison's original phonograph, the vibrations of a needle in a physical groove are mechanically translated into the physical movement of the speaker horn. With vinyl phonograph records, the movement of the stylus in the grooves is translated into an electric signal that is amplified electronically to move speakers. With compact disks (CDs), the grooves are replaced by pits in the surface of the disk that are read by a laser, much as the holes in computer cards used to be read by light beams. The signal is digital instead of analog: sound is encoded as discrete pulses instead of a continuous flow that mimics the original sound.

Magnetic storage of sound followed a similar development. With wire recording, the predecessor of tape recording, sound is converted to a magnetic signal on a thin steel wire. The wire, subject to breaks and tangles, was soon replaced with plastic tape. Sound, and later video images, are encoded as magnetic impulses on a magnetic coating on the tape. One has only to repackage the tape as a small plastic or metal disk to create the floppy disks and hard drives of computers.

The final electronic storage device of import is the memory chip, a chunk of silicon capable of storing electronic signals in digital format.

THE COMPUTER AGE

The ability to store electronic signals provided a critical prerequisite for the computer revolution. The technology originally developed to store sound could store words and numbers.

Texts could now be translated into electronic signals. Letters, once written in pencil or ink on a piece of paper, would be input into a computer from a keyboard. As was the case with writing and printing earlier, electronic books could be stored and retrieved, sent and received. *Filing a document* would no longer suggest paper and a file cabinet; electronic memories, floppy disks, and hard drives would take the fore. Checking a book out of the library would evolve into downloading a file from a remote computer.

Handwritten margin notes:
- Phonograph reproduction
- Sound storage
- Wax cylinder
- Vinyl phonograph
- Magic storage of Sound
- Memory chip
- of the hard work for future. and also NOW.
- How does Computer age work?
- Texts into electronic signals
- letters input into computer from a keyboard.
- the ability to store electronic signals provide a critical prerequisite for the computer revolution.
- store words and numbers

ELECTRONIC IMAGES

Discussions of computers often focus on numerical manipulation. They find the origins of computers in the early mechanical calculating machines and in the development of microprocessing chips. Our concern, however, is with words rather than numbers, with writing rather than calculating. From this perspective, the final precursor technology of note was popularized with the television set: the cathode ray tube provided a visual display for electronic signals.

As we shall see in the next chapter, the Internet arose from efforts to transmit stored text and images across an electronic network. Advances in the Internet in future years lie with the development of means of exchanging greater amounts of data in a shorter period of time, whether by cable television, fiber-optical cable, or satellite, and by the extension of the network to incorporate other forms of communication.

- The origin of computer was found in the early Mechanical Calculating machines. and in the development of Microprocessing chips

Concern - Words not numbers
   - Writing " calculating

The Cathode ray tube — Visual display for electronic signals.

3

Bulletin Boards, On-line Services, and the Birth of the Internet

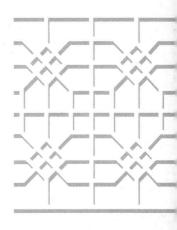

The historical survey in the previous chapter brings us to the 1960s. Telephones are in place nationwide. Television is the rage. Computers are large machines serviced by technicians, churning out mailing lists and calculations in the basements of major institutions.

Initially, each computer sat alone. For computers to communicate with one another, a person had to physically carry punched cards or computer tape from one computer to another.

By the 1970s, time sharing allowed additional terminals to be added, much like extension phones on a telephone line. A number of keyboards and monitors could communicate with a central computer, but there was still essentially only one computer.

In the ensuing decade, manual labor increasingly gave way to machines and machines gave way to electronics. The business office was transformed. Personal (that is, desktop) computers replaced the typewriter and adding machine, the file cabinet and card catalog, and the possibility of true networks emerged.

A computer network is simply two or more connected computers. If one computer provides a particular service for another, it is called a server, and the user a client. Computers may be permanently wired together within an office or by leased lines, or they may be connected intermittently by telephone line. As early as the 1970s, business communication was transformed by local area networks (LANs) within offices and wide area networks (WANs) spanning the country.

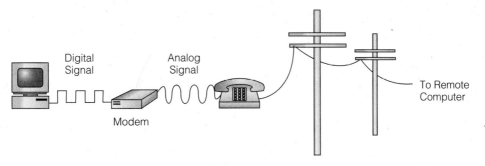

FIGURE 3.1   Modem Conversion Between Digital Computer Signal and Analog Telephone Signal

THE MODEM

The largest existing communications network available to computers is the telephone system. Computer communication over a telephone line is made possible by a device called a modem (Figure 3.1). Modems extended the reach of individual computers beyond office walls.

Modems translate the digital signal generated by a computer to an analog signal capable of transmission over normal telephone lines. Modems also dial and execute the commands necessary for establishing a viable connection. The screech heard when one computer initially contacts another is, in a wonderful turn of phrase, the modems handshaking to recognize a common transmission speed and a common communications language.

BULLETIN BOARDS

Once modems became available inexpensively in the 1980s, enterprising computer operators hooked their computers to telephone lines and offered files and information to anyone who called. Then they went further. They allowed people to post announcements and personal mail on the central computer. They offered chat sessions for callers to discuss issues with anyone else connected at the time. Part party line and part computer library, bulletin board systems (BBS) formed a new medium for personal communication.

The bulletin board movement continues to be driven by individual computer enthusiasts (system operators, or sysops). There may be as many as one hundred thousand bulletin boards in the United States today, with some seventeen million users.

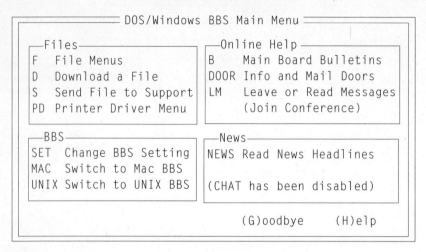

```
═══════════════ DOS/Windows BBS Main Menu ═══════════════
┌─Files────────────────────────┐ ┌─Online Help──────────────┐
│ F   File Menus               │ │ B    Main Board Bulletins │
│ D   Download a File          │ │ DOOR Info and Mail Doors  │
│ S   Send File to Support     │ │ LM   Leave or Read Messages│
│ PD  Printer Driver Menu      │ │      (Join Conference)    │
└──────────────────────────────┘ └──────────────────────────┘
┌─BBS──────────────────────────┐ ┌─News─────────────────────┐
│ SET   Change BBS Setting     │ │ NEWS Read News Headlines  │
│ MAC   Switch to Mac BBS      │ │                           │
│ UNIX  Switch to UNIX BBS     │ │ (CHAT has been disabled)  │
└──────────────────────────────┘ └──────────────────────────┘
                                     (G)oodbye    (H)elp
```

FIGURE 3.2   Opening Menu of WordPerfect Bulletin Board*

Bulletin boards tend to focus on specific regions or interest areas. There are bulletin boards for hobbyists, musicians, sports fanatics, political and cultural groups, singles, religious groups, and senior citizens. Local and national bulletin boards provide a means of outreach for many charities and for self-help and support groups. There is a Handicap News BBS (Shelton, Connecticut), a Gay and Lesbian Information Bureau (Arlington, Virginia), and a Choice in Dying BBS (New York).

Most bulletin boards are free. All that is required to use them is a computer with a modem and basic communications software. Others, especially those offering a specific service or serving a national audience, may require minimal membership dues. Almost all have user-friendly menu systems, and many utilize color (see Figure 3.2).

Bulletin boards have been put to use for commercial purposes. Companies, especially in the computer industry, provide bulletin boards for product announcements and technical support. The New School for Social Research in New York City offers adult education courses via a bulletin board that includes lectures, class discussion, assignments, and instructor feedback—although they might prefer to describe this as educational telecommunication rather than as a bulletin board.

*Here, as in a limited number of cases throughout the book, examples of text-interface screens have been edited slightly to fit the physical dimensions of the page.

```
                         ═════════ Main Menu ═════════
 ┌────────────────────────────────────────────────────────────────────┐
 │                                                                      │
 │  1.  User Account Information    6.  BBS News                        │
 │  2.  News and Information        7.  How Can We Serve You            │
 │  3.  Economic Data                    Better?                        │
 │  4.  State and Federal Grants    R.  Read Your Mail                  │
 │  5.  Taxability Information       X.  Exit System (Logoff)           │
 │                                                                      │
 │     Select an option:                                               │
 │                                                                      │
 └────────────────────────────────────────────────────────────────────┘
```

FIGURE 3.3   Opening Menu of Texas State Comptroller's Office Bulletin Board

Commercial companies also use bulletin boards for their own purposes. Apple employees communicated via AppleLink. Domino's Pizza established Domilink, a private bulletin board system, among the eleven thousand workers at its twenty-eight North American distribution sites to relay recipes, cooking protocols, and company news. — *information*

Government and public institutions have also taken advantage of the user-friendly nature of bulletin boards. Iowa was the first state to link government, education, justice, and medical institutions with fiber-optic cable, forming the Iowa Communications Network. The Texas Information Highway and Maryland Sailor system both offer access to state agency bulletin boards, federal government documents, and resources of the Internet itself (see Figure 3.3).

More than a hundred federal government bulletin boards can be reached via FedWorld, (703) 321-3339. FedWorld (Figure 3.4) includes the full text of select government publications, statistical files, job listings, satellite images, and more.

The National Public Telecomputing Company, a grass-roots coalition of business and community leaders formed in 1984, has created Freenet bulletin board systems offering business, government, and educational resources free of charge in more than fifty cities.

As with previous modes of communication, bulletin boards are linked together into wider networks. Files on some bulletin boards are copied (echoed) onto other systems. Postings to discussion groups are linked through FidoNet (so named allegedly because the software program was such a dog to write). CRIS, a bulletin board of bulletin boards, was recently formed to link bulletin boards across the country by high-speed cable so that they might all be available anywhere for a local call.

```
Min online today: 0 minutes      Time per day: 180 minutes

  ┌─┐ ┌─┐ ┌─┐ ┌┐┌┐ ┌─┐ ┌─┐ ┌─┐
  FEDWORLD

          National Technical Information Service
   A  Help and Information Center (READ FIRST)
   B  Locate and Reference Government Information
   C  Business, Trade and Labor Mall
   D  Health Mall
   E  Environment and Energy Mall
   F  Regulatory, Government Administration and State Systems
   G  Research, Technical and Education Mall
   J  Federal Job Openings
   L  Alphabetical Listing of All Information Online
   M  FedWorld MarketPlace
  [T] Forums   [U] Utilities/Files/Mail   [X] Goodbye (logoff)
             96 other user(s) online now.

  Hot command => /go MAIN
  Please select an option from above and press <return>:
```

FIGURE 3.4   Opening Menu of FedWorld Bulletin Board

Bulletin boards have played a historic role in the development of computer communication. Many of the services initially begun on bulletin boards are available in expanded form on the Internet. Bulletin boards have also had an influential role in shaping computer culture. They have provided the model for the openness and informality that characterized the early Internet. Today, bulletin boards remain a convenient means by which newcomers can initially dip a foot into the ever-expanding stream of network communication.

ON-LINE SERVICES

Local bulletin boards and national single-purpose bulletin boards were soon followed by national on-line services, which are essentially commercial bulletin boards. By mid-1995, prior to the launch of the

Microsoft Network, close to nine million people were enrolled with on-line services, with many enrolled in more than one service. Of the major on-line services, CompuServe and America Online (see Figure 3.5) had roughly three million subscribers apiece, Prodigy 1.6 million. By year's end, 10 percent of all U.S. households would subscribe to an on-line service.

As suggested, on-line services, unlike most bulletin boards, are commercial ventures rather than community resources. They require formal membership and passwords. Monthly membership charges are generally on the order of $10 for anywhere from five to ten hours and an additional $3 to $5 an hour on-line fee thereafter. Some services impose additional surcharges for the use of certain databases, such as the stock market reports, airline reservations services, or some news services. Some charge more for the use of faster modems, use during prime-time hours, or access via an 800 number.

On-line services are independent networks with their own programs and features. Some, like CompuServe, are aimed at commercial customers. (CompuServe offers its own Visa Gold Card with on-line access to account information.) Some, like Delphi, are based on providing Internet access. Prodigy, America Online, and Apple's eWorld are more family-oriented (see Figure 3.6). Strictly commercial on-line services such as Dialog/DataStar offer databases for lawyers (Criminal Justice Abstracts), doctors (Medline), and business (Business Wire) at substantially higher monthly and on-line fees. Lexis/Nexis, a full-text legal/news/business information service with seven hundred thousand subscribers, offers access to five hundred million documents!

Consumer oriented on-line services typically provide the following:

- Access to news services
- Discussion groups for personal and special interest areas
- Financial information, including real-time or delayed stock market information
- Computer files
- Research materials such as encyclopedias
- Games
- Travel and lifestyle resources
- Some form of electronic mail service

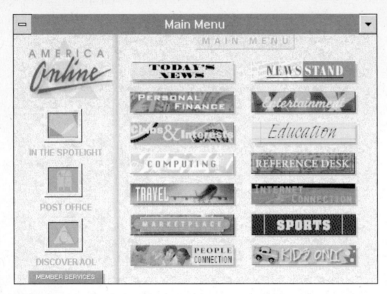

FIGURE 3.5   Opening Menu of America Online Service

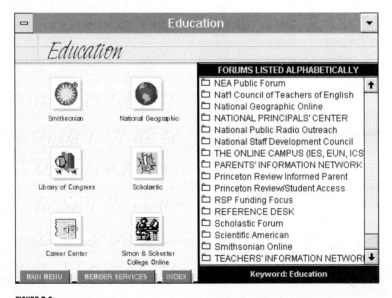

FIGURE 3.6   Education Menu from America Online Service

While most of the services offered are similar to those of bulletin boards, they are more comprehensive. Almost all on-line services provide a graphic interface that is more user-friendly than the text-based graphic that is screens of most bulletin boards. By early 1995, all of the major on-line services offered access to most programs on the Internet.

ARPANET, NSFNET, AND PACKET SWITCHING

In the late 1960s, as the story has it, researchers at the U.S. Defense Department's Advanced Research Projects Agency sought to tie computer facilities in California and Utah into a network that would be immune to potential disruption by natural or military disaster. According to others, they simply sought a more efficient means of transferring data between computers using different computer languages. In any event, they designed a network on which information was packaged in a number of small, fixed-length electronic envelopes or packets. Programs along the route read the addresses and forwarded each packet on its way. Packets from different messages could share the same line and packets in a single message might travel different routes. The original file would be reconstituted at the other end. As long as packets were addressed properly, they would find their way around broken cables or failed systems. ARPAnet was thus formed–and with it the basis for the Internet.

Who's Calling?

Like everyone else, computer operators like to know who's calling. Whether you call a bulletin board, an on-line service, or a computer on the Internet, you will be asked to identify yourself. This involves both a name (userid or username) for identification purposes and a password for verification. Some bulletin boards automatically call you back to at least verify your phone number. Systems with unrestricted access may ask for a username of "new" or "guest" or, as with some Internet services, "anonymous."

In 1986, the National Science Foundation established a network (NSFnet) of supercomputer hubs for scientific research. All communication was directed to one of five central locations that in turn were connected to each other, much like the hub system of airlines. This network was soon connected to ARPAnet. In time, NSFnet was extended to researchers and students in all disciplines and later to private companies. NSF provided the major network cables or backbone.* Regional support was provided by consortium networks and local support by individual educational and research institutions.

ARPAnet's use of "packet switching" technology was revolutionary in more than a technological sense. It would have significant social and political implications.

Bulletin boards and on-line services both involve individual subscribers communicating through a central facility. Everything emanates from the center as do the spokes of a wheel. Mail is sent to the central computer where it is retrieved by the intended recipient. Files are uploaded to the central computer where they are available to individual subscribers. The physical layout of the network provides control of the network. Whoever controls the center controls what comes in and goes out, what is available and what is not. This concept is illustrated in Figure 3.7.

*The network is still there, but it is now in commercial hands. See Part Four, "Issues."

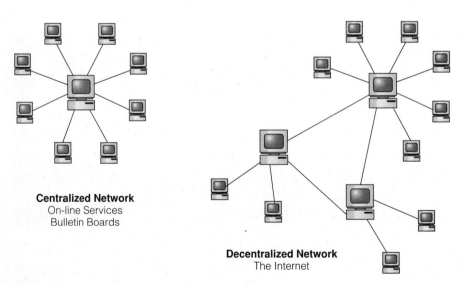

Centralized Network
On-line Services
Bulletin Boards

Decentralized Network
The Internet

FIGURE 3.7   Centralized Versus Decentralized Networks

With packet switching, networks took on a new configuration. The image changes to that of a web or, according to some computer scientists, a cloud. Everyone can send mail directly to anyone else. Anyone can make files available to anyone else. The initial character of the Internet as a cooperative environment for free scholarly discussion was thus established. The physical structure of the network inspired, and implied, democracy. (For further discussion, see Part Four, "Issues.")

THE INTERNET

In time, the network created by ARPAnet and NSFnet grew to include other university and governmental networks. The resulting inter-network evolved into the Internet.

We can think of the overall matrix of computers connected to the outside world as constituting cyberspace. As Figure 3.8 suggests,

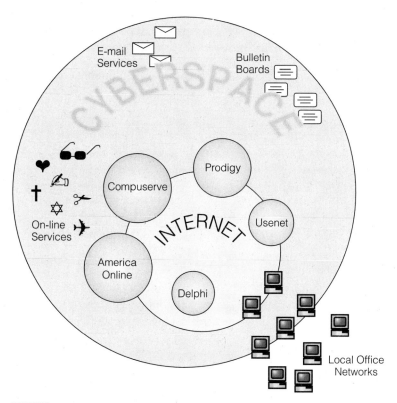

FIGURE 3.8 The Matrix of Interconnected Computers

Bulletin Boards, On-line Services, and the Internet Compared

	Bulletin Boards	On-line Systems	Internet
Coverage	local/national	national	international
Sponsor	nonprofit	profit	nonprofit
Policy Set by	operator (sysop)	corporate owner	users
Special Software	none required	proprietary	commercial or public domain
Cost Estimate (many higher)	free	$10/month + hourly fee after 6 hours	$15/month + hourly fee after 15 hours
Primary Use	information, communication, entertainment	entertainment, communication, business	communication, academic research, business, entertainment

Note: These are general tendencies of each system,
not necessarily adhered to in all cases.

many of these networks are interconnected or overlapping. The Internet is a significant, but not all-encompassing, subset of cyberspace as a whole.

As much as anything else, the Internet is characterized by the use of a common language: TCP/IP–Transmission Control Protocol/Internet Protocol, a language first used on the ARPAnet in 1983. For practical purposes, the best test for Internet participation is whether or not a computer can access the major Internet services: telnet, Gopher, World Wide Web, and so on, as compared to simply receiving mail or news services.

The Internet is run by a variety of entities collaborating as consortium parties. It is overseen by the Internet Society, a loosely affiliated group of volunteers with offices in Reston, Virginia. A number of Network Information Centers (NICs) provide users with documentation, guidance, advice, and assistance.

Roads are supported by tolls and taxes. The post office runs by selling stamps. The cost of maintaining the Internet has been borne basically by connection fees at each level and by relatively small government subsidies to major centers forming the physical backbone of the system. Individual access accounts typically cost about $200 a year. A large university may pay up to $100,000 a year to connect to a regional carrier.

Statistics on the Internet are notoriously suspect and changing every day. Differences in statistics often reflect disagreement as to what the Internet truly encompasses. Some count those with Internet access through on-line services; some don't. Some count every computer on an office network connected to the Internet; some include only those users who actually access the Internet. So the debate goes on.

Rough figures are nevertheless easy to come by, and by any means of measurement the growth has been astronomical. In 1981, the Internet consisted of about two hundred hosts, computers linked to the Internet with a specific address. By mid-1995, that number was around five *million*, with roughly thirty million individual users (Figure 3.9). In a stunning example of outrageous extrapolation, the Internet Society estimated that at the 1995 growth rate, every person in the world will have access to the Internet by the year 2003!

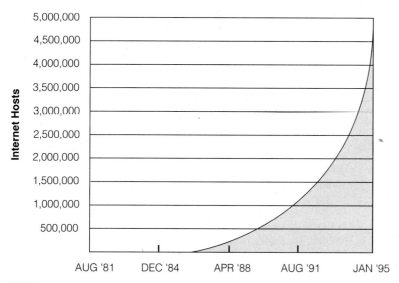

FIGURE 3.9   Growth of Internet Hosts

> "World Wide Web Frequently Asked Questions
> (FAQs)," a periodic discussion of the World Wide
> Web, warns:
> In all cases, regard this document as out of date. De-
> finitive information should be on the Web, and static
> versions such as this should be considered unreliable
> at best. The most up-to-date version of the FAQ is the
> version maintained on the Web.

Roughly 25 percent of the Internet users are based in educational institutions, 20 percent in commercial enterprises, and 4 to 5 percent in government or military institutions. In early 1995, complete Internet links existed in more than sixty countries, as major activity rapidly extended beyond the English-speaking world (United States, Canada, England, and Australia).

Future expansion worldwide is dependent of course on the availability of infrastructure resources, especially a viable national telephone system. The Internet remains in constant evolutionary change. For a survey of current issues and future concerns, see Part Four, "Issues."

 ## The Internet Index

Win Treese publishes a monthly listing of Internet statistical trivia inspired by the "Harper's Index" *(http://www.openmarket.com:80/ info/internet-index/current.html).*

The Internet Index, Number 6, 12 February 1995

Estimated number of people who can use interactive services on the Internet: 13.5 million

Percentage of movie ads with Internet addresses in the *Boston Globe* on 12 February, 1995: 8

Number, per day, of Prodigy users registering to use Prodigy's World Wide Web access: 15,000

Price, per hour, of World Wide Web access on Prodigy after the first five hours: $2.95

Average time, in minutes during business hours, between registrations of new domains: 2

Cost of access, per minute, to Internet services at Cybersmith [a new store in Cambridge, Massachusetts]: 17.5 cents

Cost, per cup, of cappuccino to enjoy while surfing: $2.00

Percentage increase in number of Internet hosts from October, 1994 and January, 1995: 26

Percentage increase in number of registered domains from October, 1994 and January, 1995: 28

Number of Norwegian television shows with a WWW home page: 1

Number of financial service firms with registered domains: 398

Percentage increase in the number of financial service firms with registered domains during 1994: 197

Estimated number of Usenet sites, worldwide: 260,000

Estimated number of readers of the Usenet group rec.humor.funny: 480,000

Percentage of WWW users who are single: 53

Percentage of Australian homes with a personal computer: 25

Number of regional networks acquired by Bolt, Beranek, and Newman: 3

Rank of TOPTEN, a mailing list about David Letterman's Top Ten list, among LISTSERV mailing lists: 1

Number of subscribers: over 27,000

Annual fee, in pounds, of dialup access to the Internet with British Telecomm: 1750

Percentage of Estonian elementary and secondary schools connected to the Internet: 16

Estimated number of U.S. newspapers offering interactive access: 3,200

Estimated number of jobs that would be created under proposed deregulation of the telecommunications industry: 1.4 million.*

---

*Reprinted by permission of Win Treese.

II

The Internet

4

Some Internet Basics

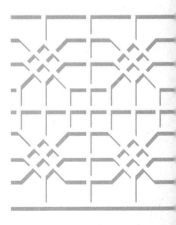

Y ou do not have to be a rocket scientist to use the Internet. For all practical purposes, the basics of Internet use reflect everyday activities involving the telephone, the post office, and basic computer operations.

INTERNET PROVIDERS

To use the telephone, you need an account with–and a connection to– a telephone company. (The connection would normally be by wire, but it could also be by radio, as with cellular telephones.) To be "on the Internet," you need to be connected to an Internet service provider, a computer already connected to the Internet. The provider will usu- ally be either a commercial company that you access by telephone or a computer network within an office or institution. Either provides a gateway or on ramp to the larger network itself. (For further discus- sion of the options, see Appendix B, "Getting on the Internet.")

INTERNET ADDRESSES

Just as every house has a street address, every account on the Internet is assigned a unique address.

Post office addresses divide the world into physical regions: houses on streets, in towns, in cities. Internet addresses indicate com- puters on networks within networks. Each level of the network is re- ferred to as a domain.

The computer running the file transfer protocol (FTP) program (see Chapter 10) at the National Center for Supercomputing Applications (NCSA) at the University of Illinois at Urbana-Champaign (UIUC) has the address *ftp.ncsa.uiuc.edu.* This is the Internet way of indicating a particular computer (*ftp*) at a particular center (*ncsa*) within a larger university network (*uiuc*). The final abbreviation indicates the nature of the account, here an educational institution (*edu*). The most common final domain names include the following:

- *edu*–educational institutions
- *gov*–government institutions
- *com*–businesses or Internet service providers
- *mil*–military sites
- *net*–administrative organizations of the Internet
- *org*–other organizations

Foreign addresses have an additional two-letter country abbreviation at the end, as in *ftp.nsysu.edu.tw,* which is the address of the FTP program at the National Sun Yat Sen University (*nsysu*) in Taiwan (*tw*).

Many individuals may live in the same house and have the same street address. Similarly, various individual users may access the Internet from the same provider and hence from the same address. For this reason, the address of an individual user consists of a username and a domain address:

user	@	*address*
username	at	domain address

The username and domain address together make up a complete Internet E-mail address. The author of this book, accessing the Internet from the Internet provider *moontower.com,* might have the address *dkurland@moontower.com.*

> ## Internet Protocol Addresses
> All alphabetic addresses have a numerical equivalent, an Internet Protocol (IP) address, in computer language, as it were. IP addresses consist of four numbers separated by dots. The notation 141.142.20.50 is the same address as *ftp.ncsa.uiuc.edu.*

THE COMMAND PROMPT

To use the Internet, access your Internet provider and sign in with a username and password. What happens then varies depending on how you are connected to the Internet. In most cases, you will either be confronted with a menu of services or with an Internet prompt similar to the DOS prompt (C:>) requesting a specific command. In the latter case, the prompt often contains the name of your provider (such as Moontower%). This is simply a command prompt in the UNIX operating system language common to many Internet programs. On local networks, you might find the generic Internet prompt: telnet%.

Once you access a specific program, you are presented with a prompt for that program, such as that for the Archie program: archie>.

When you exit an Internet program, you once again reach the provider prompt. You can then logoff to end the session.

UNIFORM RESOURCE LOCATORS (URLs)

Each document on the Internet (that is, on a host computer connected to the Internet) can be located through the use of a uniform resource locator (URL). URLs indicate a number of major items:

- the protocol for accessing the document
- the address of the computer on which that document is located
- the path to that document through a sequence of Web pages, menus, or subdirectories
- where applicable, the name of the file

URLs have this form:

protocol:// address / file path / filename

Consider an example:

http://www.clark.net/pub/listserv/listserv.html

The first part of the address specifies the means of access, here *http*, Hypertext Transfer Protocol, associated with the World Wide Web (see Chapter 14). The information immediately following the double slash indicates the address of the computer (server*) to be accessed:

*Since the host computer is providing a service to another computer, it is a also a server in a server-client relationship.

www.clark.net. Terms following single slashes indicate the path, here a sequence of pages on the World Wide Web: */pub/listserv.*

Finally, there is a specific filename, *listserv.html,* recognizable by the period within the name and the *html* ending indicating a page in the Hypertext Markup Language (again, see Chapter 14).

Other URLs look like this:

- telnet
  telnet://dra.com
- newsgroup
  news://alt.hypertext
- file transfer protocol
  ftp://wuarchive.wustl.edu/mirrors
- Gopher
  gopher://spinaltap.micro.umn.edu/1/fun
- World Wide Web
  http://info.cern.ch:80/default.html

Programs that direct you to a directory rather than a specific document (as with ftp, above) do not include a filename. Newsgroup files are on a network that is accessed independently by all computers (hosts), hence no domain address is needed. Note also that in the last example the server address (*info.cern.ch*) includes a port number (*:80*).

The next chapter introduces the general, all-purpose Internet program telnet and offers charts outlining the programs considered in the remainder of this book.

Note to the Reader

Every effort has been made up to the time of publication to assure the accuracy of addresses offered here. Internet addresses, however, like everyday addresses and phone numbers, can change and be discontinued. If an address fails, try again later, or use one of the search programs (Chapter 16) to find a current address.

Responses to frequently asked questions (FAQs) covering all aspects of the Internet are available from

ftp://rtfm.mit.edu/pub/usenet-by-group/
news.answers/Internet-services/faq or
http://www.cis.ohio-state.edu/hypertext/faq/usenet/FAQ-List.html.

There are FAQs for almost everything, especially newsgroups:

ACEDB Genome Database Software FAQ

AIDS FAQ part 1 of 4: Frequently Asked Questions with Answers

alt.fan.monty-python FAQ

Anonymous FTP Frequently Asked Questions (FAQ) List

Cancer–Online Information Sources FAQ

Common Questions and Answers about Veronica, a title search and retrieval system for use with the Internet Gopher

Creating Newsgroups

Economists' Resources on the Internet

FAQ: Computer Security Frequently Asked Questions

FAQ: How to Find People's E-mail Addresses

FAQ: Internet-Zugaenge in Deutschland

Fleas, Ticks, and Your Pet: FAQ

Gopher (comp.infosystems.gopher) Frequently Asked Questions (FAQ)

Historical Costuming FAQ

How to Read Chinese Text on Usenet: FAQ for alt.chinese.text

Journalism Resources on the Internet

On-Line Providers

Pagemaker FAQ

soc.religion.quaker Answers to Frequently Asked Questions

Usenet Primer

Welcome to news.newusers.questions! (weekly posting)

5

Telnet

The Internet

as Remote Control

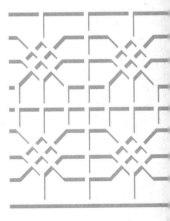

Here we begin a survey of the programs available on the Internet. We start with the most general, the plain vanilla operation of simply gaining access to another computer. The program for doing this is called telnet.

Overview

Your keyboard, computer, and monitor are connected to each other with wires. If those wires are extended, you can run your computer from a distance. If those wires are extended from your computer to another computer, you can access the files of the remote computer. The keyboard and screen are your own, but you are using another computer.

In most cases, you access another computer for a specific purpose. You go there to use a particular program suited to a particular task or to examine files unavailable elsewhere. Other than for sending and receiving mail, time spent on the Internet generally involves accessing files or browsing from menu to menu or searching via search programs. Any data manipulation or real creativity is generally done alone on our own machine, "off-line" as it were.

Remote control of another computer is hardly new with the Internet. You run another computer when you dial up a bulletin board or participate on an office network. What *is* different is the number of possible activities and the physical range of computers available to you.

USING TELNET

Upon gaining access to the Internet, simply type: **telnet** and an address.*

Moontower% **telnet archie.rutgers.edu**

This example is from a computer using an Internet provider named Moontower. The address is for a computer at Rutgers University that provides public access to a program called Archie.

The telnet program automatically contacts the computer at that address (using the numerical IP address),

Trying 128.6.18.15...

waits for a response, and reports its status.

Connected to dorm.Rutgers.EDU.
   Escape character is '^]'.
   SunOS UNIX (dorm.rutgers.edu) (ttys3)

When a connection is established, another prompt requests a username:

login:

Select a service by giving the name of that service as your username.

login: **archie**

What happens now depends on where you've "telneted" to. In this case, we've accessed the Archie program. Upon login, the Archie server sends some basic housekeeping information:

Last login: Sat Jan 28 20:35:48 from dayton.wright.ed
SunOS Release 4.1.3 (TDSERVER-SUN4C) #2:
   Mon Jul 19 18:37:02 EDT 1993
Bunyip Information Systems, 1993, 1994
Terminal type set to 'vt100 24 80'.
'erase' character is '^?'.
'search' (type string) has the value 'sub'.

The host concludes with a prompt for an Archie command:

archie>

The Archie program is now available.

---

*Here, as elsewhere throughout this book, user input is in boldface. Less important material is indented slightly for clarity.

With the Archie server, no password is required. In this case, you have opened on a prompt. On other occasions, you might open on a menu of choices.

The telnet command is used to access real-time chess (*telnet://chess.onenet.net 5000*) and backgammon games (*telnet://fraggel65.mdstud.chalmers.se 4321*) as well as adventure and role-playing games such as Galactic Bloodshed, Empire, and Multi-User Dungeons (MUDs). In January 1995, Dr. Robert Lowenstein, an astronomer at the South Pole, used telnet to manipulate a telescope in New Mexico, eight thousand miles away. With only an ordinary desktop computer, he was able to receive images minutes later–and to turn off the lights in the observatory in New Mexico when he was done.

Most of the activities of the Internet can be accomplished using the telnet command at public access sites. The telnet command is important then as a means of executing programs otherwise unavailable on your own machine. If you don't have a particular program, access a computer that does with the telnet command.

INTERNET SERVICES

Internet services involving communication include the following:

- Electronic mail (E-mail)
- Mailing lists (discussion groups and newsletter subscriptions)
- Newsgroups
- Talk and chat groups

Internet activities involving accessing data include the following:

- File transfer protocol (FTP)
- Browsing Gopher menus
- Archie and Veronica searches
- Wide Area Information Server (WAIS) searches
- Browsing the World Wide Web

The lists on the next page summarize the discussion that follows.

What Each Internet Activity Yields

E-Mail Programs

E-MAIL	personal correspondence
MAILING LISTS	subscriptions to public correspondence
NEWSGROUPS	posted letters and other files

Browse Programs

GOPHERS	access to resources at other locations
WORLD WIDE WEB	hypertext pages with links to resources at other locations

Retrieval Programs

FTP	files to download or read
WAIS	documents to download or read

Search Programs

	Input	Output
ARCHIE	file name	location of file
VERONICA	topic	a menu of Gopher resources
WAIS	key terms	documents containing key terms

(The World Wide Web includes programs for key term and topic searches of all resources of the Internet.)

What You See on the Screen

E-MAIL	letters
MAILING LISTS	letters, newsletters, etc.
NEWSGROUPS	announcements, articles, files, etc.
FTP	directories of files
ARCHIE	lists of files and their locations
GOPHER	topic-oriented menus and menus of documents
VERONICA	Gopher menus
WAIS	database directories and documents
WORLD WIDE WEB	hypertext pages

All of these services require programs written for the specific purpose. (Some programs may cover more than one service.) These programs may be loaded onto your computer, accessed along with access to the Internet itself, or accessed at specific Internet sites.

Hytelnet

Hytelnet, a database of telnet-accessible sites that is updated regularly, is available by file transfer protocol (FTP) at *ftp://access.usask.ca/pub/hytelnet/* in DOS, UNIX, and Macintosh versions.

6

Electronic Mail (E-mail)

The Internet

as Post Office

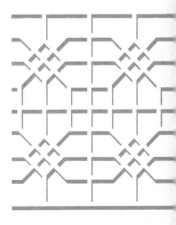

In 1995, the novelty underwear manufacturer Joe Boxer replaced its toll-free customer number with an electronic mail (E-mail) address, asking customers to "Contact us in underwear cyberspace." This was more than an advertising ploy to suggest that the company was up with the times. Thirty to forty million people in more than 160 countries have at least E-mail access to the Internet. America Online, only one of many commercial on-line services, processes roughly 350,000 messages *daily*. The U.S. Postal Service estimates that one-third of the mail among businesses since 1988 is carried by fax and E-mail over the Internet and commercial services.

OVERVIEW

Computer networks are used primarily to send and receive mail. To send regular mail ("snail mail," to Internet users), you go to the post office or mailbox. To send E-mail, you hit a key or click on an icon.

Are You on the Internet?

Contrary to popular belief, the ability to E-mail does not necessarily indicate that you are on the Internet. Electronic mail can also be sent on local office networks, commercial mail networks, or bulletin board networks. Even if you can E-mail to an Internet address, that might be the limit of your Internet access.

Stamps? With E-mail, the only fee is the price of the phone call to your Internet provider.

In many ways, E-mail is truly revolutionary. For a start, the traditional impediments of "neither snow, nor rain, nor heat, nor gloom of night" are irrelevant. E-mail on the Internet travels anywhere in the world in minutes, not days. Two or more people can send a document back and forth for revision across thousands of miles as though their desks were next to each other.

E-mail contains both a return address and a subject heading, so that recipients can decide whether or not to read a message right away. E-mail often offers a direct route to people otherwise inaccessible. When you are having trouble getting through on the phone: E-mail. Can't get past a secretary? E-mail.

In other respects, however, little has changed. You still have to have something to say to someone, and you still have to know that person's address. There is still the excitement of discovering that you have mail—and still the nuisance of wading through junk mail. Finally, mail is still delivered by being passed on from one location to another until it finally arrives at its destination.

While the Internet delivery system can overcome many problems, it is not foolproof. Lines may be down or computer systems may be out. Excessive traffic may slow access to a particular location—and even the Internet cannot surmount an incorrect address. E-mail may report back unknown addresses and problems with delivery, but regular mail is more forgiving of simple errors in addresses.

Surfing the Internet by E-mail

All of the services of the Internet can be accessed via E-mail—albeit often in a very limited manner. For complete instructions, see "Accessing the Internet by E-mail, Doctor Bob's Guide to Offline Internet Access." The document can be obtained by sending an E-mail letter to *listserv@ubvm.cc. buffalo.edu.* Leave the subject blank and limit the body of the letter to

get internet by-email nettrain f=mail

Parts of an E-mail Letter

The following example illustrates the various sections of an E-mail letter. Note especially the routing information in the header.

HEADER

```
From ajjksrl   Fri July 28 18:00:00 1995

Received: from peabody.car.com (peabody.car.com
[140.120.5.1])
   by beacon.moontower.com (8.6.5/8.6.5) with SMTP id
   QAA03363
   for <dkurland@moontower.com>; Wed, 26 July 1995
   12:32:18 -0500

Received: from KurlandJJ.car.com
   by peabody.car.com (AIX 3.2/UCB 5.64/4.03) id AA11824;
   Wed, 26 July 1995 13:35:18 -0400

Date: Wed, 26 July 1995 13:35:18 -0400
Message-Id: <9505192126.AA11824@peabody.car.com>
Mime-Version: 1.0
Content-Type: text/plain; charset="us-ascii"
```

ADDRESS

```
To: dkurland@moontower.com
From: ajjksrl@peabody.car.com (Jon Kurland)
```

SUBJECT

```
Subject: standard message
```

BODY OF TEXT

```
Dan

I just got back from seeing Rachel in Vermont. The weeping
willow is doing fine. Looking forward to seeing you in June.

Jon
```

SIGNATURE

```
Jonathan J. Kurland
CAR Corporation
ajjksrl@peabody.car.com
```

Using E-Mail

E-mail must be addressed to a person or entity, not to a computer. E-mail addresses thus have the form: *user@address.* When a computer has only intermittent access to the network, mail is stored by the network provider. This latter practice is common with on-line services and bulletin boards.

Once you have read ordinary mail, you have a number of options. You might save it to reread, throw it in the wastebasket, or file it away as unfinished business. Much the same options are available with an E-mail program.

E-mail programs are part word processor, part mailbox, and part file organizer. You may

- delete an item from the list of documents received
- print a copy for later reference
- save a document as a file on your computer.

In addition, you can

- store frequently used names and addresses
- automatically attach "signatures," special comments, or simply your name and address, at the end of letters
- send replies automatically
- include portions of the original message in a reply to clarify your responses
- forward mail to someone else by simply readdressing it
- list mail received and mail sent
- attach other files to mail.

Some programs will alert you to arriving mail whatever you are doing on your computer at the time, provided you have uninterrupted access to the Internet.

Finally, copies of a document can be sent to any number of people at once, a feature that facilitates the traditional telephone tree and fosters the proliferation of both jokes and junk mail over the Internet.

LITZLER

"HE HAS E-MAIL BUT NOTHING TO SAY."

Source: Reprinted by permission of Mark Litzler.

Signatures

Signatures often serve the function of a letterhead. They may be purely informational, such as that of one of the leading computer information periodicals:

```
*************************************************************
Cybernautics Digest * 3530 Bagley Ave. N. * Seattle, WA 98103
Voice: 206/547-4950 * Fax: 206/545-2294
* E-mail: twhansen@cuix.pscu.com
World Wide Web: http://www.pscu.com/cyber.html
*************************************************************
```

At times, they are more artistic, such as that of Eric W. Tilenius, author of the "Complete Guide to Cows!"–a collection of drawings using typographical characters:

```
        (__)      Eric W. Tilenius
        (oo)
 /----------\/    President, Princeton Planetary Society
/ ||        ||
* ||-------- ||   609-734-7677 // ewtileni@pucc.Princeton.EDU
  ||        ||
```

Text Versus Graphic E-mail Programs

Since E-mail programs vary widely and are fairly intuitive in their operation, we shall not indicate commands for specific E-mail programs other than to note that the standard text-interface programs (mail, pine, and elm) are not particularly user-friendly. Yet here, as elsewhere, the command **?** or **help** will usually provide a list of commands whatever program you are using. A graphic-interface program such as Eudora, which is available for both Macintosh and Windows systems (see Figure 6.1), greatly simplifies the processes.

Social Aspects of E-mail

E-mail encourages the regular exchange of short communiqués. You do not have to hunt for paper, envelopes, and stamps. No special preparation is necessary.

While E-mail messages seem to exist ephemerally on the screen, you must take care not to commit anything to electronic mail that you would not want committed to written form. E-mail can be read by

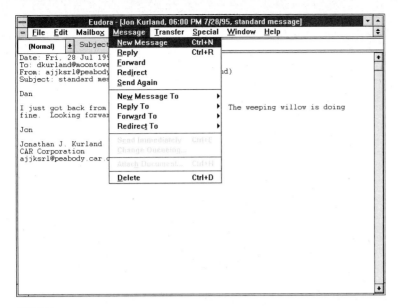

FIGURE 6.1 Message Options on Graphic-interface E-mail Program

others on a network, and any mail you send to one person may be forwarded intact to others without your permission. And with E-mail, as with other forms of correspondence, care must be taken not to be unnecessarily vague, ambiguous, or suggestive. Sarcasm and humor must be used cautiously to avoid misunderstandings.

Ever resourceful, E-mail users both speed their task and qualify their remarks with acronyms such as BTW (by the way), IMHO (in my humble/honest opinion), FWIW (for what it's worth), and OTOH (on the other hand). Words are stressed by enclosing them in *asterisks*.

Ever playful as well, E-mail writers have also developed a series of symbols (emoticons) to replace voice inflection and facial expressions in their letters. The most famous of these symbols is the smiley, a key-board-written image indicating delight with an idea:

:-).

Other smileys include

:-(upset or depressed about last comment or issue

:-J   tongue-in-cheek comment

¦-)   sarcastic or joking

Official acceptance of emoticons was signaled on May 21, 1995, when the *New York Times* Sunday crossword puzzle included clues such as 8(:o) and I8-#)""–obviously Mickey Mouse and Groucho Marx!

Users of the Internet constitute their own subculture, one that has definite standards of fair play and respect for others (netiquette). One should not YELL BY WRITING EVERYTHING IN CAPITAL LETTERS nor forward mail to large groups of people (spamming).

The discussion above has focused on one-to-one correspondence and variations on that theme in which personal mail is forwarded to one or more people. The next chapter examines other ways in which the technology of electronic mail can be utilized.

Finding Addresses

Since there is no definitive Internet, there is no definitive directory of names and addresses. There are however a number of search programs examining portions of the system.

The Knowbot Information Service (KIS), based at the Internet Society in Virginia (*telnet://info.cnri.reston.va.us*), searches various directory services to find street address, E-mail addresses, and phone numbers.

The best way to learn a person's E-mail address is still to call the person on the telephone, or ask someone else.

7

Mailing Lists, Newsgroups, Talk and Chat

The Internet

as Bulletin Board,

Bull Session,

and Party Line

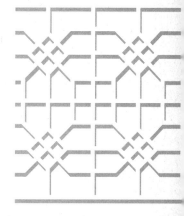

Mention the mail service and one might first think of personal correspondence—of love letters, birthday cards, and letters from Uncle Marty saying the family will arrive tomorrow with the German schnauzer. In reality, of course, our mailboxes are often filled with mass mailings, appeals for charitable donations, advertisements, professional newsletters, and magazines. Electronic mail, like regular mail, is multipurpose.

MAILING LISTS: AN OVERVIEW

Earlier, we noted that a single E-mail message can be directed to any number of people at once. The same process can direct subscriptions to newsletters or electronic magazines to people around the globe. Individuals subscribe by E-mail and in return receive material periodically—again, E-mail. (Nonsubscribers can usually request individual items from the mailing list via E-mail.) "Hotflash," the weekly newsletter of *Wired* magazine, claims over one hundred thousand subscribers, increasing at the rate of five hundred a day.

In some instances, subscription mailing lists are administered by an individual. In many cases, the administrative duties are conducted by a computer. The server computer automatically reads and responds to requests to start, stop, or pause subscriptions. Such servers are called, appropriately, listservers. The major program for administering mailing lists is, again appropriately, *listserv*. A sure sign that a mailing list is administered by machine is that the contact address refers to *listserv*, or one of a number of alternative programs such as *majordomo* or *listproc* at a particular address.

Talking to Machines

The notion of automated mail programs can prove eerie or amusing, depending on your perspective. The following message was received in response to a blank E-mail message sent to *gopher-news-daemon@boombox.micro.umn.edu.*

```
From: "Dream Police"<gopher-news-daemon@boombox.micro.umn.edu>
To: dkurland@moontower.com
Subject: Huh? Your request was not understood.
Status:

Hello,

This is the daemon caretaker of
gopher-news-request@boombox.micro.umn.edu. I accept subscribe
or unsubscribe requests for gopher-news.

I could not find either the word "subscribe" or "unsubscribe"
in your message. I am not a listserv. I am dumb and only
have a vocabulary of two words. So I'm returning your mail
clipped below.

To subscribe to gopher-news, send mail containing the word
"subscribe" to gopher-news-request@boombox.micro.umn.edu.

To unsubscribe from gopher-news, send mail containing the word
"unsubscribe" to gopher-news-request@boombox.micro.umn.edu.

If something isn't working and you need to talk with a human,
send email to gopher@boombox.micro.umn.edu.
```

USING MAILING LISTS

Since all mailing list activities involve E-mail, the only software required to participate on mailing lists is an E-mail program. Administrative tasks are accomplished by single word commands. To subscribe to the "HotFlash" mailing list, you simply E-mail to

info-rama@hotwired.com

with the message

subscribe hotflash

in the body of the letter. If you get more verbose, the server will reply with a list of appropriate commands.

The exact commands vary with the particular server involved. An E-mail letter with the single word *help* in the body of the letter will usually evoke a reply with a list of appropriate commands. Finally, most mailing list messages will contain an E-mail address of an actual human being to contact if the need should arise.

DISCUSSION GROUPS: AN OVERVIEW

With subscription mailing lists a single person or central authority regularly produces documents for distribution to subscribers. Listserver programs then automate the subscription and distribution process.

Listservers, however, have additional capabilities. The same program that sends out periodic mailings to subscribers can also forward correspondence from one subscriber to all other members of the mailing list. The result is a discussion group much like an electronic bull session or giant party line. Subscribers receive a copy of all communi-

---

Useful Subscription Mailing Lists

- "Internet Index": list of Internet statistical trivia
  (*internet-index-request@OpenMarket.com;*
  subscribe internet-index)
- "Net Happenings Digest": announcements from InterNIC
  Information Services (*majordomo@dsmail.internic.*
  net; subscribe net-happenings-digest)
- "The Scout Report": a weekly report of Internet activities
  (*majordomo@dstest.internic.net;* subscribe scout-report)

---

cations sent to the group, whether sent by a subscriber or not. Such groups are referred to alternately as discussion groups, electronic mailing groups, or, just to confuse matters, mailing lists. Alternatively, they are labeled by reference to the computer managing the group: listservers.

Some discussion groups forward all correspondence; some are moderated by an individual to assure the relevancy of the discussion; some incorporate messages into a periodic newsletter. Some groups are open; some have membership restrictions (via password).

More than thirteen thousand listserver discussion groups are active. Since the system had its origins on academic networks, many listservers are associated with academic organizations, associations, and societies.

USING DISCUSSION GROUPS

Subscriptions to discussion groups are handled in much the same way as are mailing lists. You must, however, distinguish between the address of the server that administers the distribution of messages and the address of the discussion group itself. Send subscriptions to the first address, messages to be distributed to the second.

Discussion groups about recent computer programs function as on-line user-to-user technical support networks. The following letter about the World Wide Web browser Cello was forwarded to all subscribers by *cello-l@listserv.law.cornell.edu*. (The name has been changed to protect the privacy of the sender–something which would not be done in the discussion group itself.)

```
From Gail Goldman    Jan 28, 95 08:07:41 am EST
Date: Sat, 28 Jan 95 08:07:41 EST
   Errors-To: owner-cello-l@listserv.law.cornell.edu
   Reply-To: cello-l@listserv.law.cornell.edu
   Originator: cello-l@listserv.law.cornell.edu
   Sender: cello-l@listserv.law.cornell.edu
   Precedence: bulk
To: Multiple recipients of list
<cello-l@listserv.law.cornell.edu>
Subject: Getting information through the Listserv?
X-Listprocessor-Version: 6.0c—ListProcessor by Anastasios Kotsikonas
   X-Comment: Support List for the Cello Internet browser
```

Hi, I am trying to get more information on CELLO, so that I can understand how it is set up and used with WINSOCK (which I don't understand either). I subscribed to read the messages and see if others were asking the same questions as I. Can someone tell me how to get some of the files available, because I don't quite understand the information which came with the program.

I have the Cello-1 help file and have tried to ask for an "index", even a "list", from the listserv@listserv.law.cornell.edu. I have even used the "Get" command with these requests. All have been returned.

Thank you one and all for your time.

Gail

Gail Goldman
Internet: ggoldman@bluemail.net

Private replies: ggoldman@bluemail.net
Public replies: cello-1@listserv.law.cornell.edu
To subscribe, signoff, to digest: listserv@listserv.law.cornell.edu
Other housekeeping:
owner-cello-1@listserv.law.cornell.edu

Note the difference between the final three addresses:

- the user's personal E-mail address for private replies
- the group's E-mail address for messages to be distributed
- the E-mail address of the administrative server for subscription commands

Finally, be forewarned: provocative news items can trigger a deluge of comments from an ever increasing membership. Since each subscriber receives *all* correspondence, hundreds of letters may suddenly appear in your mailbox!

Notice also that the message is short, precise, and polite–as it should be if it is being sent to hundreds of strangers.

Finding Discussion Groups

The document "Publicly Accessible Mailing Lists" is posted on the 19th of each month. It is available on the Usenet newsgroup *news.answers* or by anonymous file transfer protocol from *fpt://rtfm.mit.edu/pub/usenet-by-group/news.answers/mail/mailing-lists.*

A selected listing can be obtained by E-mail from *listserv@ubvm.cc.buffalo.edu* with the message

list global /*modifier*

where *modifier* indicates a specific search term within titles or descriptions.

Alternatively, you can examine a complete listing with search and subscription capabilities at the World Wide Web site *http://scwww.ucs.indiana.edu/mlarchive* (see Figure 7.1) or with the InfoMagnet program at *http://www.clark.net/pub/listserv/imag.html.*

 ## Sample Mailing Lists

The descriptions reflect the wording of mailing list owners.

Anesthesia and Critical Care Resources

A resource discovery forum for discussion of Gophers, World Wide Web (WWW), and telnet sites, software, documents, and so forth, on anesthesiology, critical care, pain management, and related areas, as well as for distribution of the list owner's document, "Anesthesia and Critical Care Resources on the Internet."

Antiquaria

A subscription mailing list expressly for rare book dealers to exchange information and books amongst each other and to meet with individuals and institutions looking for specific books.

Ballroom Dancing

An unmoderated mailing list for the discussion of any aspect of ballroom and swing dancing.

The Catholic Approach to Christianity

A forum for Catholics who wish to discuss their discipleship to Jesus Christ in terms of the Catholic approach to Christianity.

Computer Privacy Digest

A moderated mailing list dedicated to the discussion of how technology impacts privacy.

Higher Ed Database

A resource in which individual people interested in and knowledgeable about higher education issues are described in a succinct and consistent format that facilitates networking and searches for expertise.

Himalayan Earth Science

A moderated mailing list for geologists and/or geographers working in the Himalayan countries of Pakistan, India, Tibet (China), Nepal, and Bhutan.

Namibian Network List

A moderated mailing list to discuss initially the technical aspects of electronic networking in Namibia but also any other topic relating to Namibia.

Navy News Weekly

The weekly *Navy News Service* (NAVNEWS), published by the Navy Internal Relations Activity in Washington, distributed through Navy circuits to ships at sea and to shore commands around the world, containing official news and information about fleet operations and exercises, personnel policies, budget actions, and more.

Russian History 1462–1917

A forum for discussion of any aspect of the history of Russia from the reign of Ivan III (1462–1505) to the end of the Romanov dynasty in the person of Nicholas II (1894–1917).

White House Health Plan

A mailing list as a conduit through which the White House sends health-reform announcements directly to health professionals and others with electronic mailng addresses.

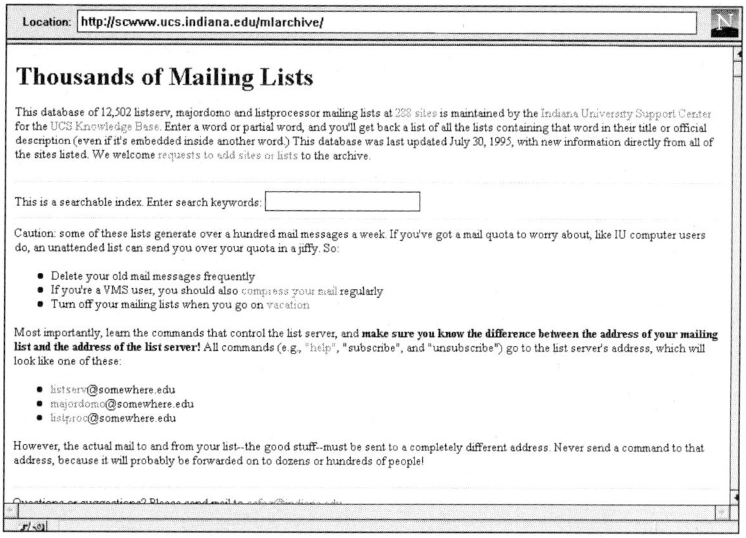

Thousands of Mailing Lists

This database of 12,502 listserv, majordomo and listprocessor mailing lists at 288 sites is maintained by the Indiana University Support Center for the UCS Knowledge Base. Enter a word or partial word, and you'll get back a list of all the lists containing that word in their title or official description (even if it's embedded inside another word.) This database was last updated July 30, 1995, with new information directly from all of the sites listed. We welcome requests to add sites or lists to the archive.

This is a searchable index. Enter search keywords: [   ]

Caution: some of these lists generate over a hundred mail messages a week. If you've got a mail quota to worry about, like IU computer users do, an unattended list can send you over your quota in a jiffy. So:

- Delete your old mail messages frequently
- If you're a VMS user, you should also compress your mail regularly
- Turn off your mailing lists when you go on vacation

Most importantly, learn the commands that control the list server, and **make sure you know the difference between the address of your mailing list and the address of the list server!** All commands (e.g., "help", "subscribe", and "unsubscribe") go to the list server's address, which will look like one of these:

- listserv@somewhere.edu
- majordomo@somewhere.edu
- listproc@somewhere.edu

However, the actual mail to and from your list—the good stuff—must be sent to a completely different address. Never send a command to that address, because it will probably be forwarded on to dozens or hundreds of people!

Questions or suggestions? Please send mail to refer@indiana.edu

FIGURE 7.1 World Wide Web Site for Searching for and Subscribing to Mailing Lists

NEWSGROUPS: AN OVERVIEW

Mailing list and discussion group messages are E-mailed to individual subscribers. Newsgroups combine the ability to publicly post documents on a specific topic with possibilities for personal discussions. Newsgroup messages are posted for anyone to read and respond to. They combine the impersonal postings of mailing lists with the person-to-person interchange of discussion groups.

Newsgroups are posted on Usenet. Usenet is not technically an Internet program but rather a separate worldwide network set up in 1979 with Duke University as its central hub. Usenet newsgroups provide an international town forum by which people can gossip, debate, and discuss shared interests, a conferencing system by which people from all walks of life can inform, argue with, query, and harangue each other. A large portion of the Usenet traffic is now carried by the Internet.

Seven categories of newsgroup postings are distributed worldwide: "news," "soc," "talk," "misc," "sci," "comp," and "rec." There are in addition subcategories that are limited to a specific institution or geographic area. In addition, there is an "alt" category, a miscellaneous heading for anything that does not fit elsewhere, "biz" for business-related groups, and "gnu" for groups related to the GNU Project of the Free Software Foundation.

Anyone with a special newsreader program can read and respond to postings on more than ten thousand active newsgroups. Anyone can download files, ask questions, or simply "listen in" on the electronic conversations. Newsgroups are often used to distribute the latest versions of FAQs (frequently asked questions) relating to popular software or any other interest area.

Sample Newsgroup Headings

"alt"—nontraditional or alternative viewpoints on all topics

alt.amazon-women.admirers

alt.fan.nancy-kerrigan.ouch.ouch.ouch

alt.food.sushi

alt.sports.football.pro.dallas-cowboys

alt.tv.dinosaurs.barney.die.die.die

"comp"—computer science, software, hardware, and systems

comp.doc.techreports

comp.graphics.research

comp.sys.ibm.pc.games.adventure

comp.sys.ibm.pc.games.flight-sim

comp.sys.mac.misc

"misc"—themes not easily classified under other headings

misc.education.adult

misc.forsale.computers.pc-clone

misc.kids.health

misc.invest.funds

misc.jobs.offered

misc.kids.pregnancy

misc.rural

"rec"—the arts, hobbies, and recreational activities

rec.arts.theatre.musicals

rec.arts.marching.band.high-school

rec.autos.sport.indy

rec.collecting.sport.basketball

rec.food.preserving

rec.games.computer.doom.playing

rec.pets.dogs.breeds

"sci"—research or applications of the established sciences

sci.geo.oceanography

sci.lang.translation

sci.physics.accelerators

"soc"—social issues and socializing

soc.culture.indian.telugu

soc.culture.malaysia

soc.genealogy.surnames

soc.college.gradinfo

soc.couples.intercultural

soc.culture.african.american

"talk"—debate-oriented topics

talk.bizarre

talk.politics.drugs

talk.politics.mideast

talk.religion.newage

talk.rumors

Source: Copyright 1995 John Deering.
Reprinted with permission.

USING NEWSGROUPS

Each newsgroup contains collections of postings or articles that are essentially E-mail messages. Postings on the same topic are assembled into "threads."

Usenet readers (the programs, that is) typically allow each user to subscribe to a specific set of groups from a list of three to four thousand available on any single network. Other newsgroups can still be retrieved, but the system does not have to load all of the messages when starting. The result is a personal menu.

The following is an example using the text-interface newsreader **tin.**

```
Moontower% tin
    tin 1.2 PL2 [UNIX] (c) Copyright 1991-93 Iain Lea.
Reading news active file...
Checking for new newsgroups...
Subscribe to new group alt.fan.tarantino (y/n/q) [n]:
Checking............

Group Selection (15 R)

1      8777    news.newusers.questions
2      21      austin.announce
3      4329    austin.general
4      1410    austin.jobs
5      34      austin.food
6      16      austin.eff
7      11      austin.news
8      15      austin.public-net
9      927     rec.music.classical
10     945     alt.winsock
11     3723    comp.sys.ibm.pc.misc
12     234     comp.windows.x
13     112     comp.binaries.ibm.pc.d
14     11      comp.binaries.ms-windows
15     113     comp.windows.misc

<n>=set current to n, TAB=next unread, /=search pattern,
c)atchup,g)oto, j=line down, k=line up, h)elp, m)ove, q)uit,
r=toggle all/unread, s)ubscribe, S)ub pattern, u)nsubscribe,
U)nsub pattern, y)ank in/out
```

The number in the second column indicates the number of articles available in that group at that time. (The large numbers here result from the fact that this is a new account.) You can purge articles after reading them and limit yourself to recent postings. Any article that you have read will not reappear unless intentionally marked as unread.

The most used commands actually involve the cursor keys. Move up and down to select an item from the menu; use the right and left arrow keys to enter or leave each level. Placing the cursor on the group *news.newusers.questions* in the menu above and hitting the enter key or right cursor arrow produces the following list of postings in that group:

```
1    +      Member Name or alias           Shelby Syckes
2    + 2    Help with questions            Phil Edwards
3    +      How to Offline read            Dave Balcom
4    +      NNTP Service Needed            Elwood2
5    +      New Group                      MGiordani
6    +      Finding info                   Los
7    +      ONLINE LIBRARY?                David DeLaney
8    +      post message                   David DeLaney
9    +      I need help re:Ad for Book sale  David  DeLaney
10   + 2    E-mailing                      Bill Marcum
11   +      Where are the CFRPG's?         David DeLaney
12   +      test -- disregard              Bruce Heling
13   +      GIF/JPG - Downloading & Converting  David DeLaney
14   +      ?NEED AMNESTY-I e-mail ADDRESS  David DeLaney
15   +      TST                            David DeLaney
16   + 2    Html files                     Bill Marcum

<n>=set current to n, TAB=next unread, /=search pattern,
^K)ill/select, a)uthor search, c)atchup, j=line down,
k=line up, K=mark read, l)ist thread, ¦=pipe, m)ail,
o=print, q)uit, r=toggle all/unread, s)ave, t)ag, w=post
```

This is only the first 16 of the 8,777 postings indicated. In the above example, the single-digit number before the posting title indicates the number of articles in a thread of responses. The + indicates that the thread has not yet been read. (Since this represents a new account, none have been read.)

As you may notice, there are numerous commands to save or print a file, search for a particular term, mark files as read, or go to the next article in a thread of responses or respond with a new posting within the thread, directly to the author of an article, or with a totally new posting. Programs usually include word processing/E-mail capability (or access to such programs) to facilitate the posting of responses. All newsgroup files are in text mode; graphics and sound files must be decoded prior to viewing (see Appendix A).

As with E-mail programs earlier, graphic-interface programs rely on a point and click approach instead of specific commands (see Figures 7.2 and 7.3).

NEWSGROUPS: PERSPECTIVE

Usenet groups are at once the essence and the bane of the Internet. As you can well imagine from the earlier list, the level of discussion can vary from the intellectual to the puerile, from mainstream to radical. While some newsgroups are moderated for content, discussion is generally uncensored, encouraging a range of belief and expression with which many are uncomfortable.

As the forum for the freest expression on the Internet, newsgroups are often subject to restrictions or outright censorship. Many Internet providers do not carry some or all of the comp.binaries groups (binary files often containing provocative graphic images). Some sites take only a selected subset of the more technical groups, and controversial "noise" groups are not carried by many sites. Administrators have restricted student access to newsgroups on university networks, an action that has evoked inevitable controversy.

Of all sites on the Internet, newsgroups are the preferred venue for uninhibited surfing and lurking, technical terms for scanning and reading without responding. For what it's worth, a report of a day's

---

Finding Newsgroups

Access to the Usenet network includes access to the hundreds if not thousands of newsgroups carried by your particular Internet provider. Indexed archives (excluding alt.*, soc.*, and talk.*) are available on the World Wide Web at *http://www.dejanews.com*, and "Interest-Groups," a listing of Usenet newsgroups, is available by file transfer protocol from *ftp://usc.edu/net-resources.*

newsgroup usage from the University of California, Santa Cruz, showed the following:

ucsc.messages	1,975
alt.binaries.pictures.erotica	290
alt.sex.stories	110
ucsc.baskin.general	146
ucsc.cats.d	102
ucsc.class.cmp101	109
ucsc.baskin.grad	81
scruz.general	77
rec.humor.funny	51
scruz.events	45
ba.market.computers	43
scruz.market	42
alt.binaries.pictures.erotica.amateur.female	39
alt.binaries.multimedia.erotica	35
ucsc.class.cmp112	31
alt.fan.letterman.top-ten	30
alt.binaries.pictures.celebrities	23

Readers may draw their own inferences, if any.

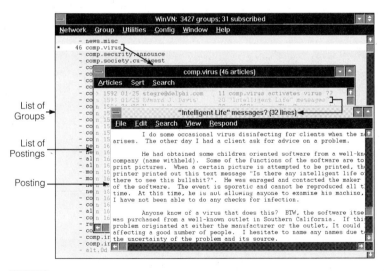

FIGURE 7.2   Newsgroup Posting Viewed with Graphic-Interface Program WinVN

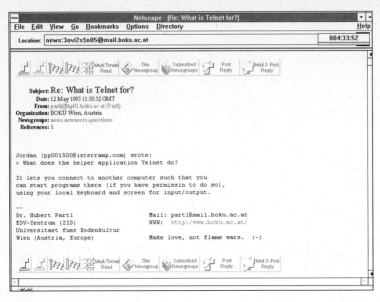

FIGURE 7.3   Newsgroup Posting Viewed with World Wide Web
Browser Netscape

 ## Newsgroup Etiquette

Chuq Von Rospach's "A Primer on How to Work With the Usenet
Community" on *news.newusers.questions,* a guide to using the
Usenet politely and efficiently, concludes with the following:

Summary of Things to Remember:

Never forget that the person on the other side is human.

Don't blame system admins for their users' behavior.

Never assume that a person is speaking for their organization.

Be careful what you say about others.

Be brief.

Your postings reflect upon you; be proud of them.

Use descriptive titles.

Think about your audience.

Be careful with humor and sarcasm.

Only post a message once.

Please rotate material with questionable content.

Summarize what you are following up.

Use mail, don't post a follow-up.

Read all follow-ups and don't repeat what has already been said.

Double-check follow-up newsgroups and distributions.

Be careful about copyrights and licenses.

Cite appropriate references.

When summarizing, summarize.

Mark or rotate answers or spoilers.

Spelling flames considered harmful.

Don't overdo signatures.

Limit line length and avoid control characters.

Please do not use Usenet as a resource for homework assignments.

Please do not use Usenet as an advertising medium.

Avoid posting to multiple newsgroups.

TALK AND CHAT PROGRAMS: AN OVERVIEW

Talk and chat programs got their start on local bulletin boards. Talk programs allow two people to "talk" by typing remarks back and forth without exiting their screens. They offer text-based on-line communication. Chat programs are simply group talk programs. They work somewhat like citizens band radio. Participants can often choose from a list of available chat groups. They can enter or exit a discussion at will, identified only by a handle or nickname they have selected.

USING TALK AND CHAT PROGRAMS

Internet talk programs can be initiated at the provider prompt with a **talk** command and an E-mail address. The recipient, assuming he or she is on-line at the time, receives an on-screen message indicating that a session has been initiated. The recipient has only to respond with the same command and the appropriate return E-mail address. A newer program, ntalk ("new talk," of course), is also available.

The Internet version of a chat program is called Internet Relay Chat (IRC). Originally written by Jarkko Oikarinen in 1988 in Finland, it has spread to over sixty countries around the world.

Internet Relay Chat requires special software. (For further information, see the newsgroup: *alt.irc*). The first person to initiate a channel acts as the operator with various administrative duties, including the duty to exclude unruly participants. Individual servers may have thousands of channels at one time. As many as ten thousand users may be on hundreds of channels at only one time during the day. Calls can be private or public, among friends, family, or business associates.

IRC programs have proven invaluable for joining large numbers of people at times of crisis, such as after the terrorist bombing in Oklahoma City. On the other hand, Figure 7.4 suggests that the discussion is not always scintillating. The illustration depicts discussion on the general chat channel #*friendly* on an alternative IRC network, Under-Net, (*http://www2.undernet.org:8080/cs93jtl/Undernet.html*). Other channels include #*chessland* (a games channel), #*slovenija* (a foreign channel), #*Christians* (a religious channel), #*AynRand* (a philosophy channel), and #*Podium* (a live talk show channel Wednesday nights at 9 P.M. CST, U.S.).

New chat programs reflect the general evolution of the Internet toward increasingly sophisticated audio and graphics programs–and with that, a requirement for faster and faster computers, modems, and sound boards.

An experimental World Wide Web version of chat called WebChat (*http://www.irsociety.com/wbs.html*) includes photographs of participants (Figure 7.5). Worlds Chat (*http://www.worlds.net/wc/welcome.html*) goes WebChat one better, providing a virtual three-dimensional room with photographs of the participants, and Global Chat (*http://www.prospero.com/globalchat*) allows you to add both sound and graphics clips to an otherwise text-based chat session.

Add real-time voice and chat programs will mimic telephones. Internet Phone *(http://www.vocaltec.com)* enables real-time voice conversations between two people. CUSeeMe (*http:/magneto.csc.ncsu.edu/Multimedia/classes/Spring94/proj6/cu-seeme.html*) allows real-time voice and video conferencing utilizing the Internet.

U.S.A. IRC Servers

irc.bu.edu	mickey.cc.utexas.edu
irc.colorado.edu	irc.virginia.edu

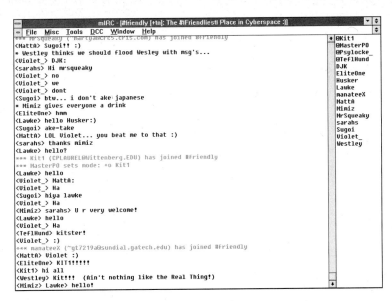

FIGURE 7.4 Discussion on Internet Relay Chat Channel *#friendly*

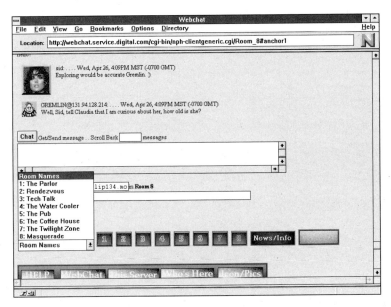

FIGURE 7.5 Discussion on Webchat Channel *Masquerade*

8

File Transfer Protocol

The Internet

as Lending Library

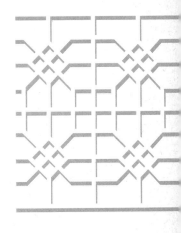

INTRODUCTION

Libraries contain more than books. They are archives for photographs and phonograph records, manuscripts and government documents, newspapers and academic journals, financial reports, employment listings, oral history tapes, and recipe collections.

All of the materials traditionally stored in a library can be stored in electronic form. "We live in a world today," Raymond Kurzweil has noted, "in which all of our knowledge, all of our creations, all of our insights, all of our ideas, our cultural expressions–pictures, movies, art, sound, music, books, and the secret of life itself–are all being digitized, captured, and understood in sequences of ones and zeroes."* And anything archived can be accessed.

Not so long ago, you would go to the library to research a topic. You would search through the card catalog, go to the shelves, look for specific books or other materials, peruse an index for a specific topic, and read or copy the desired information. With the Internet, you can do the complete process without leaving your desk.

The old model was of books on the shelves of libraries or papers in folders in file cabinets. The new model is not much different–only the physical nature of the items has changed. Text encoded on files is stored in directories and subdirectories within computer memory. Instead of going to a building to get information, you "login" by computer and telephone wire.

*Raymond Kurzweil, Keynote, Second U.S./Canada Conference on Technology for the Blind.

The above scenario presupposes two circumstances: (1) that the appropriate material has been entered into computers and (2) that you can gain access to those files. As luck would have it, this is just the case—and more so every day!

The Internet offers a number of approaches to accessing archived materials. You might visualize each in terms of library research:

- **file transfer protocol (FTP)**

  selecting a library (computer) and going from floor to floor (directory to directory) and shelf to shelf (file to file) in search of specific documents

- **Gopher**

  browsing from one document in one library to another document in another library

- **Wide Area Information Servers (WAIS)**

  searching for specific terms in documents at one or more libraries

An additional approach, the World Wide Web (WWW), integrates all three and adds additional elements all its own. Each approach is examined more closely in the following chapters, starting here with FTP.

OVERVIEW

FTP is a procedure for reading and copying files on remote computers. It works like a lending library, but you get to keep the book!

You cannot willy-nilly tap into *any* computer, nor can you access *everything* on a specific computer. The computer in question must be connected to the network and must grant public access to the desired directories and activities. (The remote computer must in other words act as a server to your computer as client.) Computers that grant public access to selected directories are said to offer anonymous file transfer. Roughly three thousand sites provide anonymous FTP service. Two-thirds of these sites are in the United States, and three-fifths of those are located at educational institutions.

File transfer is a major activity on the Internet. The anonymous FTP program at the Center for Innovative Computer Applications at Indiana University, a clearinghouse for Microsoft Windows programs, offers access to 1 1/2 gigabytes (1,500,000,000 bytes) of public Windows-related files. It receives fifty thousand logins a month requesting 70 gigabytes of data.

Obviously, traffic such as this can tie up the lines. To ease the problem, other sites "mirror" copies of the relevant files. The trick is to call a site that gets less action or to call when the local time is not during business hours. Sites that cannot respond due to heavy traffic often offer a list of mirror sites.

ACCESSING FTP

To access an anonymous FTP site with a text-interface program, enter the **ftp** command followed by the address of the desired site at the Internet provider's prompt:

Moontower> **ftp address-of-FTP-archive**

Graphic-interface programs usually allow you to maintain a directory of site addresses and descriptions. Simply select an address and the program takes it from there.

FTP Sites

A complete list of FTP sites generally serves little purpose. We have, after all, little use for a list of all of the libraries in the country; we are more concerned with knowing what books exist and where to find them. Similarly, on the Internet we are more concerned with identifying specific files and their specific location than with a long list of the locations where files might be stored. A search tool of the contents of those files is much more useful—as we shall see in the next chapter. Nevertheless, a list of anonymous FTP sites can be obtained from *ftp://garbo.uwasa.fi/pc/doc-net/ftp-list.zip*. Instruction in the use of FTP is available in the form of a Frequently Asked Questions document via E-mail from *mail-server@rtfm.mit.edu*. Include no subject and only the message:
send usenet/news.answers/ftp-list/faq

USING FTP

File search and retrieval at FTP sites is done much as it would be on your own computer. Whatever software program you employ, the sequence is the same:

1. Access the remote computer (**FTP address**).

2. Login with a username (*anonymous*) and password (your E-mail address).

3. Move from subdirectory to subdirectory with change directory (**cd**) commands to locate the desired file.

4. Read or download the desired file.

5. Repeat steps 3 and 4 as desired.

6. Logoff.

The first step, then, is to access an FTP server. In the example below, we access an FTP server at Rensselaer Polytechnic Institute in New Jersey. As always, the request for user input is initiated with a prompt of some sort. With each command, the program issues either a status report or other output.

```
Moontower% ftp ftp.rpi.edu
    Connected to netserv1.its.rpi.edu.
    220 netserv1.its.rpi.edu FTP server (SunOS 4.1) ready.
```

Once a connection is established, login with the username *anonymous.*

```
Name (FTP.rpi.edu:dkurland): anonymous
    331 Guest login ok, send ident as password.
```

Respond to the request for a password with your personal E-mail address.

```
Password: dkurland@moontower.com
230 Guest login ok, access restrictions apply.
```

The request has been accepted. As an anonymous user, you are restricted to the public-access directories.

Once accepted, you are offered the FTP prompt.

```
ftp>
```

This initial prompt is equivalent to the C : > prompt in DOS. You are at the root directory of the file directory.

The next step is to see what's there. That is accomplished with a list command. (Notice that commands and file names are usually case-sensitive–you must distinguish between capital and lowercase letters. README is different than Readme.)

```
ftp>ls
    200 PORT command successful.
    150 ASCII data connection for /bin/ls (199.170.2.1,3988) (0 bytes).
       total 11
-rw-r--r--    1  11803  wheel   730  Apr 21  1994   README.incoming
drwxr--xr--x  2  11803  wheel  2048  Apr 21  1994   bin
drwxr--xr--x  2  11803  wheel  2048  Apr 28  1994   etc
drwxr--xr--x  4  12803   4000  4096  Jan 25 20:23  incoming
drwxr--xr--x 27  12848  wheel  2048  Jan 11 21:41  pub
226 ASCII Transfer complete.
```

Note the far left column of the directory list. Names that begin with the letter *d* (for example, drwxr-xr-x) indicate subdirectories. Names beginning with a dash (as in -rw-r--r--) indicate specific files.

The number in the middle column indicates the size of the file or directory.

```
-rw-r--r--  1  11803  wheel 730     Apr 21  1994   README.incoming
```

This is followed by the date the file was last modified.

```
-rw-r--r--  1  11803  wheel 730     Apr 21  1994   README.incoming
```

The final element is the name of the file or directory.

```
-rw-r--r--  1  11803  wheel 730     Apr 21  1994   README.incoming
```

In the present example, change to the public directory, pub, and list its contents. (Access to files in other subdirectories might be available only to Rensselaer students and faculty.)

```
ftp>cd /pub
    250 CWD command successful.
ftp>ls
    200 PORT command successful.
    150 ASCII data connection for /bin/ls
    (199.170.2.1,3989)
    (0 bytes).
    total 128
```

```
-rw-------   1  25504  5086  40910  Jan 11  21:42  INDEX
-rw-r--r--   1  12803  4000  32048  Jan 27  1994   INDEX.OLD
-rw-r--r--   1  11803  wheel 389    Aug 17  1992   README
drwxr-xr-x   2  11803  wheel 2048   Jan 20  1993   anti-virus
.......................................
.............................. ...........
drwxr-xr-x   2  11803  wheel 2048   Jan 27  1994   usenet
drwxr-xr-x   2  11803  4000  4096   Jun 23  1993   workshop92
drwx------   2  25504  5086  2048   Jan 25  20:24  www
226 ASCII Transfer complete.
```

The first file indicated is a fairly large file (40,910 bytes), INDEX, presumably offering an index of the **pub** subdirectory. It is always a good policy to actually read *read.me* and *Index* files that offer additional information on the content of directories.

We can download this file to the screen to read now with the command

ftp>**get INDEX -**

or download it as a file to read later with the command

ftp>**get INDEX**
```
    200 PORT command successful.
    150 ASCII data connection for INDEX
       (199.170.2.1,3994) (40910 bytes).
    226 ASCII Transfer complete.
    41807 bytes received in 38 seconds (1.1 Kbytes/s)
```

(The "copy to screen" command has a dash; the "copy to file" command does not.) At this point, we can check out other directories and download other files—or we can quit.

ftp>**quit**
```
221 Goodbye.
```

Text-interface programs, as above, require a knowledge of a number of commands. With a graphic-interface program, each step is accomplished by clicking on a name or icon. Maneuver through directories by clicking on subdirectory names. Request files by clicking on an icon (see Figure 8.1).

Basic FTP Commands

cd/dirname	charge directory to *dirname*
cd...	change back one level higher in the directory path
dir	list files and subdirectories in detail
pwd	indicate current directory
ls	list files and subdirectories in abbreviated format
ascii	set file transfer to ASCII format (for text files)
binary	set file transfer to binary format (for program files)
get *filename*	copy the file *filename* from the server to your computer
get *filename*	read the contents of the file *filename* to the screen
hash	print pound sign (#) for every 1,024 bytes transferred to indicate network activity
help *command*	help on given command
bye, quit, exit	close connection to FTP server

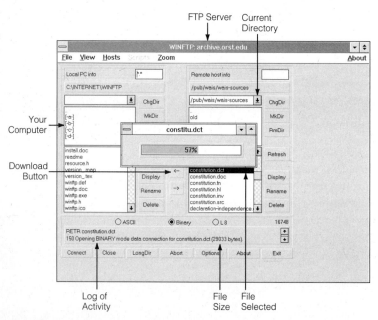

FIGURE 8.1   Downloading File *constitu.dct* with Graphic Interface File Transfer Protocol (FTP) Program

✳ FTP Netiquette

File transfer from remote computers is not a right. It is a privilege that carries with it distinct responsibilities. "The Net: User Guidelines and Netiquette," written and maintained by Arlene Rinaldi, was originally created to introduce students, staff, and faculty of Florida Atlantic University to the etiquette of the Internet. The following is a section on FTP behavior.

Anonymous Tip—File Transfer Protocol

- Users should respond to the PASSWORD prompt with their E-mail address, so if that site chooses, it can track the level of FTP usage. If your E-mail address causes an error, enter GUEST for the next PASSWORD prompt.

- When possible, limit downloads, especially large downloads (1 Meg+), for after normal business hours locally and for the remote FTP host, preferably late in the evening.

- Adhere to time restrictions as requested by archive sites. Think in terms of the current time at the site that's being visited, not of local time.

- Copy downloaded files to your personal computer hard drive or disks to remain within disk quota.

- When possible, inquiries to Archie should be in mail form.

- It's the user's responsibility, when downloading programs, to check for copyright or licensing agreements. If the program is beneficial to your use, pay any author's registration fee. If there is any doubt, don't copy it; there have been many occasions on which copyrighted software has found its way into FTP archives. Support for any downloaded programs should be requested from the originator of the application. Remove unwanted programs from your systems.*

The complete text of the guide is available at *http://www.fau.edu/rinaldi/netiquette.html.*

---

*Reprinted by permission.

As a user of FTP, you can download many freeware and share-ware programs for accessing and browsing the Internet. You can obtain copies of documents, position papers, newsletters, photographs, sound files, animated movies, and movie clips. Throughout it all, you may go from feeling like an honored guest to feeling like a cat burglar. You will be amazed at the riches available for the taking and on reflection grateful for the opportunity.

So much for *how* to look for files. But *where* should you look? That is the subject of the next chapter.

9

Archie

The Card Catalog

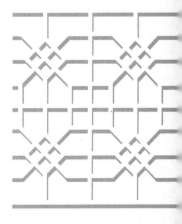

File transfer protocol (FTP) provides access to files on computers around the world—once you know where they are. But how do you know where to look for a particular file or for *any* file of a particular type? You can burrow through the subdirectories and read the indexes on one computer after another, but this is obviously both time consuming and inefficient.

As with so many aspects of the Internet, much of your information will come from word of mouth, as it were. A magazine article will mention a file. A *read.me* file for one program will refer to another program. A newsgroup posting will announce a new program. In each case, the address of a relevant FTP server will usually be supplied.

As useful as these resources may be, they will not always suffice. Some means of searching available files is still necessary. Since the Internet has no center, no central card catalog is possible. A reasonable facsimile, however, is recreated every month at a number of locations by a service and search program called Archie.

OVERVIEW

Archie (derived from the word *archive*) was developed in 1990 at the McGill University School of Computer Science. Sites that offer public access to files register with an Archie service. Over a period of a month, the Archie service scans those sites—roughly 1/30th a day—and generates a list of files and directory names at the registered sites. The resulting database is then mirrored on several other Archie servers, all of which then contain the same information.

The result is indeed prodigious! More than twelve hundred anonymous FTP sites are now represented in the Archie database, covering more than five million files.

ACCESSING ARCHIE

Public-access Archie servers are reached by the **telnet** command and a suitable address. Sign on with the username **archie** (all lowercase). No password is necessary.

In the following example, the telnet command is used to reach the Archie server at Rutgers University. Once again, user input is in bold-face. Additional information provided by the server has been indented for clarity.

Moontower%**telnet archie.rutgers.edu**

CONNECT TO SERVER

```
    Trying 128.6.18.15...
    Connected to dorm.Rutgers.EDU.
    Escape character is '^]'.
    SunOS UNIX (dorm.rutgers.edu) (ttys3)
```

LOGIN

login:**archie**
```
    Last login: Sat Jan 28 20:35:48 from dayton.
    wright.ed
    SunOS Release 4.1.3 (TDSERVER-SUN4C) #2:
       Mon Jul 19 18:37:02 EDT 1993
    # Bunyip Information Systems, 1993, 1994
    # Terminal type set to 'vt100 24 80'.
    # 'erase' character is '^?'.
    # 'search' (type string) has the value 'sub'.
archie>
```

We have reached the Archie prompt. The Archie search program is named, quite simply, "prog." Here the search is for the E-mail program Eudora.

REQUEST LOCATION OF A FILE

archie>**prog eudora**
```
    # Search type: sub.
    # Your queue position: 3
    # Estimated time for completion: 31 seconds.
    working... =0=0=0=0=0=0=0=0=0=0=0=0=0=0=0=0=0=0=0=0=0
```

The request has been entered and acted upon. The subsequent output indicates where the file Eudora is available by anonymous file transfer.

OUTPUT: LIST OF FILES AND LOCATIONS

```
Host FTP.uni-trier.de        (136.199.8.81)
Last updated 17:31 29 Dec 1994
Location: /pub/mac/info-mac/comm/net
FILE   -rw-r--r--    785635 bytes 17:00 13 Apr 1993
                               eudora-131-accessories.hqx

Host info.dkrz.de    (136.172.110.11)
Last updated 21:46 29 Dec 1994
Location: /pub/mac/net
FILE   -rw-r--r--    960108 bytes  18:00 20 Dec 1993
                               eudora-14-manual.hqx
```

....THE LIST CONTINUES.....

EXIT FROM SERVER

```
archie>quit
   # Bye.
   Connection closed by foreign host.
```

Pause to examine an example of the output:

```
Host FTP.uni-trier.de        (136.199.8.81)
Last updated 17:31 29 Dec 1994
Location: /pub/mac/info-mac/comm/net
FILE   -rw-r--r--    785635 bytes  17:00 13 Apr 1993
                               eudora-131-accessories.hqx
```

The lines above indicate

   `Host ftp.uni-trier.de (136.199.8.81)`–an FTP server, with both letter and numerical address

   `Last updated 17:31 29 Dec 1994`–the date of the last update of the Archie search

   `Location: /pub/mac/info-mac/comm/net`–the subdirectory in which the file may be found

   `FILE       -rw-r--r--    785635 bytes 17:00 13 Apr 1993`
   `eudora-131-accessories.hqx`–information on the file, including its size, much as it was presented in the FTP directory listings

The trick now is to select the most up-to-date file in the desired format at the nearest location to access via FTP. (The example above appears to be an Apple Macintosh version since it is in a public-access Macintosh directory: pub/mac.) Files are often in compressed form (indicated by extensions such as .zip or .Z; see Appendix A, "Some Computer Basics").

Note that after you submit your request

archie>**prog eudora**

many Archie servers indicate your place in line (queue position) and the expected time of completion of a search:

```
# Your queue position: 3
# Estimated time for completion: 31 seconds
```

While there are thousands of FTP servers, there are a limited number of Archie servers. Queue positions of 35 are not uncommon. If the anticipated delay is long, simply try another server. In most cases, the server will offer a list of other active servers.

As we saw earlier with FTP, text-interface programs require that you remember (or look up) specific server addresses and commands. Here again, a graphic interface simplifies the process. As with FTP programs, graphic-interface programs store lists of addresses and automatically submit the userid *archie* at the login prompt.

In Figure 9.1 an Archie server is selected from a list (*archie.ncu.edu.tw*) and the name of the desired file is entered (Eudora). Note that the search can be restricted to an exact match or to files that contain the search string, as with Eudora14.

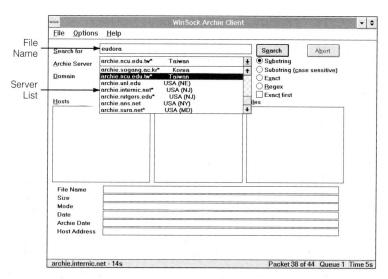

FIGURE 9.1   Selecting a File (*eudora*) and Server (*archie.ncu.edu*) for an Archie Search

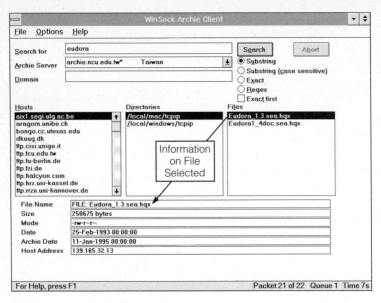

FIGURE 9.2 File Location Listings Resulting from an Archie Search for *eudora* at *archie.ncu.edu.tw*

Figure 9.2 shows the fruits of such a search. With this program, you can highlight a site (host) to display the directory and file names associated with that site in the box to the right. Details of the file highlighted in the far right column appear at the bottom of the screen.

Now you know where to find copies of Eudora. You must go back to FTP to access a copy.

WHATIS?

As described so far, Archie is fine if you know what file to look for. But that is not always the case. What if you need a Windows drawing program? What file do you look for? To help meet this need, Archie includes the "whatis" description database. This database contains descriptions and a brief synopsis for over 3,500 public domain software programs, data sets, and documents.

To search for file names, use the **whatis** command instead of **prog.** To find a drawing program, for instance, enter the command

archie>**whatis draw**

This yields the following:

cpic	A troff(1) preprocessor that produces pic(1) output; lets you draw simple graphs (nodes and edges type) in pic(1)
draw	Library of routines to produce plots in various formats and a utility that acts as a front end
fig	A MacDraw-style line editor (SunView)
kirondraw	KironDraw v2.4B
liss	Draws Lissajous figures on a Sun
muncher	Draws a "munching" pattern in a X11 window
netmap	Draws geographical maps of the world (re quires World Databank database)
pic	Draws graphical figures (SunView)
plaid	Draws plaid patterns in an X11 window
rose	A SunView program to draw "roses"
tgif	Xlib-based 2-D drawing tool (X11)
vine	Draws pictures of vines around your display (X11)
worm	Draws a window with moving "worms" in it (X11)
xfig	A MacDraw-style line editor (X11)
xgremlin	Draws figures under X11
xlmntn	Draws fractal mountains via Brownian motion (X11)
xlogo	Draws X11 logo (X11)
xmntn	Draws fractal mountains via Brownian motion (X11)
xphoon	Draws the current phase of the moon on the root window (under X11)
xpic	Draws and edits diagrams, figures, and pictures (X11)

You can now use the **prog** command to locate copies of the specific files.

The output above is hardly a list of all of the drawing programs that exist for the various computer operating systems, but it is a start. The search does not capture programs described as "graphics" or "paint" programs. Additional searches using synonyms might produce other candidates. As an alternative to using Archie, you might examine newsgroups on related topics or archives of frequently asked questions.

Basic Archie Commands

list	**list sites covered by Archie database**
prog *filename*	**search database for** *file name*
whatis *name*	**search for keyword** *name* **in database**
set search exact	**search for exact match of filename**
set search sub	**search for any file containing indicated string (sequence of letters) anywhere in the name**
help	**obtain annotated list of commands**
bye, exit, quit	**exit Archie program**
mail *e-mail address*	**send last search data to** *E-mail address*

Selected Public Archie Servers

Host	Country
archie.au	Australia
archie.funet.fi	Finland
archie.hensa.ac.uk	UK
archie.sura.ne	USA (MD)
archie.unl.edu	USA (NE)
archie.internic.net	USA (NJ)
archie.rutgers.edu	USA (NJ)

A complete, up-to-date list can be obtained via telnet from *telnet://archie.ans.net.* Login as **archie** and type **servers** at the first prompt.

10

Gopher

The Internet as

Research Library

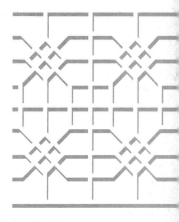

T he discussion of file transfer protocol suggested the image of going from floor to floor (directory to directory) and shelf to shelf (file to file) in a specific library (computer) in search of specific documents. You searched through directories of host computers to locate files. You focused attention on the names of files and their physical location.

Files and documents on remote computers can be organized in other ways. We can construct a menu of files in a variety of directories or on a variety of computers. From general headings, we can move to more specific headings, much as with a table of contents.

OVERVIEW

Gopher is a tool for burrowing or tunneling through resources on the Internet. In the earlier image, it is akin to browsing from a document in one library to another document in another library.

Gopher was developed by the University of Minnesota Microcomputer Workstation, Networks Center. It was released in 1991. The name is derived, depending on what you choose to believe, from either the notion of "go fer" or the university mascot, the Golden Gopher. There are about 2,500 registered Gopher servers and an estimated 7,500 in all.

Here again, you can access only what someone lets you. In this case, individual sites choose to offer access to files on their own computers. Gopher sites are for the most part located at academic institutions and government agencies. The resulting materials are therefore of an academic/research/statistical nature. Entertainment, commercial, and lifestyle resources tend to be cataloged on the more recent World Wide Web.

Gopher is based on menus. It is essentially text based, although it can be accessed with either text-interface or graphic-interface programs. The menu below is the opening menu of the "mother of all Gophers" at the University of Minnesota.

```
              Home Gopher server: gopher.tc.umn.edu
1.  Information About Gopher/
2.  Computer Information/
3.  Discussion Groups/
4.  Fun & Games/
5.  Internet file server (ftp) sites/
6.  Libraries/
7.  News/
8.  Other Gopher and Information Servers/
9.  Phone Books/
10. Search Gopher Titles at the University of Minnesota <?>
11. Search lots of places at the University of Minnesota  <?>
12. University of Minnesota Campus Information/

Press ? for Help, q to Quit,                        Page:1/1
```

The menu options cover a number of areas. You can access

• resources by topic, as with

```
2.  Computer Information/
4.  Fun & Games/
```

• resources by type, as with

```
9.  Phone Books/
```

• search programs, as with

```
10. Search Gopher Titles at the University of Minnesota <?>
11. Search lots of places at the University of Minnesota  <?>
```

• or general information, as with

```
1.  Information About Gopher/
12. University of Minnesota Campus Information/
```

Notice also the page numbering at the bottom right-hand corner of the menu. The denominator indicates the number of pages in the full menu.

Each item in a Gopher menu represents a link to files on the same or other computers. Each item in the menu above is thus associated with an Internet address and directory path:

```
            Home Gopher server: gopher.tc.umn.edu
1.  Information About Gopher/
        Host=gopher.tc.umn.edu
        Path=/Information About Gopher
2.  Computer Information/
        Host=spinaltap.micro.umn.edu
        Path=/computer
3.  Discussion Groups/
        Host=gopher.tc.umn.edu
        Path=/Mailing Lists
        . . . . . . . . . . . . . . . . . . . . . . . . .
```

Gopher menus point to other menus, which ultimately point to specific documents, whether text, pictures, animations, sound messages, files, or search programs.

Simply move the cursor down to an item and hit the enter key. The program issues a telnet, FTP, or other command to access that item, wherever it may be located. When you reach a reference to a specific file, you have only to click on that item to have that file appear before you. You can examine the outcome of your browsing at the moment or download the file for later viewing. You can see only text files, but you can download graphic and sound files for later viewing or listening.

Where Are You?

Move the cursor to one of the items (say, number 4 in the earlier example) and issue an = command, and you will obtain the address and directory associated with the server (host) for that item.

```
Name=Fun & Games
Type=1
Port=70
Path=1/fun
Host=spinaltap.micro.umn.edu
```

ACCESSING GOPHER

You can access Gopher menus in any of three ways, presented here in reverse order of preference and convenience.

If your Internet provider offers no Gopher service, you can use the **telnet** command to access any of a dozen or so public-access Gopher sites.

Alternatively, you can issue the **gopher** command without an address to access the initial Gopher menu of your Internet provider. Since all Gophers provide access to all "Gopherspace," you can get to any Gopher from any other.

Finally, you can use the **gopher** command followed by an address to reach directly to a specific Gopher site anywhere in the world. Many such Gophers are based at institutions specializing in a particular area of study and are therefore good starting points for research in the particular field.

 ## Gopher Commands

The basic commands for negotiating from one Gopher menu to another are simple. For the most part they utilize the cursor keys. You select items in the menu with the up and down cursor keys.

↑	cursor up to select
↓	cursor down to select
→, or enter key	select menu item
←	return to previous menu
PageUp	move up a page
PageDown or space bar	move down a page

If you reach a dead end, double back to an earlier choice.

Other commands include:

s	save the current item to a file
S	save the current menu listing to a file
D	download a file
/	search for an item within the menu
n	find the next search item
q	quit

Sample Gopher Menus

The following examples suggest the diversity of Gopher sites and the nature of their menus.

Texas State Legislature Gopher
gopher://capitol.tlc.texas.gov

1. About The Texas Legislative Gopher.
2. What's New in The Texas Legislative Gopher (03/17/95).
3. Texas Legislation and Legislative Information/
4. The Texas Senate/
5. The Texas House of Representatives/
6. The Legislative Branch of Government/
7. Legislative Districts/
8. Texas Capitol Information/
9. Texas Constitution/
10. Texas Internet Resources/
11. Other State Legislative Information/
12. The U.S. Congress/
13. U.S. Government Resources/
14. Gopher Jewels/
15. Other Internet Resources/
16. Internet Help/

WireTap Gopher
gopher://wiretap.spies.com:70/11/Library/Article/Language/

1. College Slang Dictionary.
2. Esperanto English Dictionary.
3. Glossary of Computer Terms in Vietnamese.
4. List of Hindu Names.
5. Meihem in Ce Klasrum: GB Shaw's proposals.
6. Mnemonics.
7. Official English: A No Vote.
8. Palindromes.
9. Qalam Arabic Transliteration.
10. Quick & Dirty Guide to Japanese Grammar.
11. Resources for Adult Learners of Welsh.
12. Small Urdu Dictionary.
13. Spoonerisms and Malapropisms.
14. Study Guide to Wheelock Latin.
15. Taeis Languages (frp).
16. Top 100 Words used on Usenet.

Daily News - Free Internet Sources Gopher
gopher://gopher.nstn.ca:70/1/Cybrary/News/news

1. About the Daily News Service
2. Global News Sources/
3. Brazil - News Service Summaries (slow!)/
4. Canada/
5. Danish News Services (Danish language)/
6. Eastern Europe/
7. France (French Language Press Review)/
8. Greece (English Audio Files)/
9. Holland (Dutch Language News)/
10. Israel/
11. Italy/
12. Poland - Gazeta Wyborcza (Polish language) <HTML>
13. Specialty News/
14. United States/

Selected Public Access Gopher Sites

Host name	Area
consultant.micro.umn.edu	North America
ux1.cso.uiuc.edu	North America
gopher.msu.edu	North America
gopher.ebone.net	Europe
gopher.sunet.se	Sweden
info.anu.edu.au	Australia
gan.ncc.go.jp	Japan

Using Gopher Bookmarks

You can create a personal menu of your favorite Gopher sites. With text-interface programs, press a to record a menu item as a bookmark, A to record the complete menu page for later recall. Pressing v invokes the bookmark menu. Bookmarks are stored in a permanent file for later use.

Text-Interface Gopher Symbols

The University of Texas offers a single menu screen containing examples of the various menu items.

1.	About this section	.	*text file*
2.	Grants and Funding	/	*additional menu item*
3.	Texas A&M directory	< CSO >	*name directory*
4.	Macintosh-Internet-cruise2.2.hqx	< HQX >	*encoded file*
5.	Windows-Internet-cruise2.0.zip	< PC Bin >	*binary file*
6.	Search CC Newsletter back issues	< ? >	*search program*
7.	Weather Underground	< TEL >	*telnet to another server*
8.	UTCAT PLUS	< 3270 >	*telnet to IBM mainframe*
9.	Monty Python: Thank you very much	<)	*sound file*
10.	Earth image, from NASA	< Picture >	*graphic file*
11.	Kandinsky: On White II	< Picture >	*graphic file*

AN EXAMPLE

The best way to get a sense of Gopher is to see it in action. One of the standard starting points on most systems is a topic-oriented menu called Gopher Jewels. The initial menu looks like this:

```
                    Gopher Jewels
1.  GOPHER JEWELS Information and Help/
2.  Community, Global and Environmental/
3.  Education, Social Sciences, Arts & Humanities/
4.  Economics, Business and Store Fronts/
5.  Engineering and Industrial Applications/
6.  Government/
7.  Health, Medical, and Disability/
8.  Internet and Computer Related Resources/
9.  Law/
10. Library, Reference, and News/
11. Miscellaneous Items/
12. Natural Sciences including Mathematics/
13. Personal Development and Recreation/
```

```
14. Research, Technology Transfer and Grants Opportunities/
15. Search Gopher Jewels Menus by Key Word(s) <?>
                                                    Page: 1/1
```

Notice the markings at the end of each line. A right slash, / , indicates that the item leads to a lower-level menu. The question mark within brackets, < ? >, indicates a searchable database.

Assume for the moment that we're interested in learning about bagpipes—not that you probably are, but the example is particularly useful for viewing a number of important aspects of Gopher. Our goal after all is to learn about Gopher, not bagpipes.

Of the choices in the opening Gopher Jewels menu above, number 13

```
13. Personal Development and Recreation/
```

seems closest to what we want. Move the cursor down to that line and press enter or the right arrow key. (Remember, we can always press the left arrow key to get back to the previous menu.)
The next screen appears:

```
            Internet Gopher Information Client v2.0.14
                 Personal Development and Recreation

1.  Employment Opportunities and Resume Postings/
2.  Fun Stuff & Multimedia/
3.  Museums, Exhibits and Special Collections/
4.  Travel Information/
5.  Jump to Gopher Jewels Main Menu/
6.  Search Gopher Jewels Menus by Key Word(s) <?>
                                                    Page: 1/1
```

Once again, we have only a single page and obviously some interesting sources to come back to some other time. But we have a job to do, so on with it. Let's try

```
2.  Fun Stuff & Multimedia/.
```

We get the following menu:

```
            Internet Gopher Information Client v2.0.14
                      Fun Stuff & Multimedia

1.  Aviation/
2.  Bicycling/
3.  Fantasy/
4.  Games/
```

```
 5. Gardening/
 6. Humor/
 7. Magazines/
 8. Music/
 9. Pets/
10. Pictures/
11. Recipes/
12. Restaurants/
13. Sports/
14. Television & Film/
15. Fun Stuff & Multimedia (misc)/
16. Jump to Gopher Jewels Main Menu/
17. Jump up a menu to Personal Development and Recreation/
18. Search Gopher Jewels Menus by Key Word(s) <?>
                                        Page: 1/1
```

All's going well. Selecting number

```
 8. Music/
```

yields the following:

```
      Internet Gopher Information Client v2.0.14
                       Music

 1. (Music Collection) - MIT/
 2. Adam Curry's Music Server (Gopher)/
 3. Alice Cooper - Western Kentucky Univ./
 4. All Music Guide (Ferris State Univ)/
 5. Bagpipe Archives - Dartmouth Col. Dept. of Comp. Science/
 6. Berkeley College of Music/
 7. Breakfast Records/
 8. Brian Behlendorf's Techno/Rave archive - Stanford Univ./
 9. CANTUS - Database for Gregorian Chants for the Divine Office Database/
10. Chinese Music - Sunsite/
11. Grateful Dead Archives/
12. Harmonica Information - Western Kentucky Univ./
13. Indian Classical Music (WAIS index @ Brown) <?>
14. Internet Underground Music Archive - Via Sunsite/
15. Internet WireTap (Music Collection)/
16. Intn'l Computer Music Assn. Software - Dartmouth Col./
17. Jewish Music - Jerusalem One Network/
18. KISSserv - Kiss Rock Group - Western Kentucky Univ./
                                        Page: 1/2
```

The wealth and diversity of the Internet should be apparent! (Are you reading all the options?) Page: 1/2 indicates that the menu continues for another page. But we have what we want, so on with number

```
5.  Bagpipe Archives - Dartmouth College Dept. of Computer Science/
```

and receive the next menu:

```
              Internet Gopher Information Client v2.0.14
Bagpipe Archives - Dartmouth College Dept. of Computer Science

1.  COCKNEY.WAV <>
2.  bagpipe-archive/
3.  bagpipe-archive-92
4.  bagpipe-archive-93
5.  bagpipe-archive-94-1
6.  bagpipe-archive-94-2
7.  bagpipe-archive-94-3
8.  bagpipe-archive-94-4
9.  bagpipe.FAQ
10. cs
11. pipe-survey
12. very experimental Indexed Bagpipe archives <?>
                                              Page: 1/1
```

We're just about there. The absence of slashes, /, indicates that we have reached individual documents. The text archives appear to be according to date. The symbol after item number 1, < >, indicates a sound file. Number 9–bagpipe.FAQ–is a frequently asked question file, a useful starting point for a new topic. Number 12 offers a searchable database.

Here again we can use the equal sign command, =, to determine the exact location of the file and additional information about it. Examining number 1, we receive the output:

```
Type=s+
Name=COCKNEY.WAV
Path=s/pub/bagpipes/COCKNEY
Host=cs.dartmouth.edu
Port=70
Admin=Wayne Cripps (603) 646-3198 <wbc@cs.dartmouth.edu>
ModDate=Fri Nov 11 09:43:25 1994 <19941111094325>
URL: gopher://cs.dartmouth.edu:70/ss/pub/bagpipes/COCKNEY
Size      Language        Document Type
____      _____   _____

639k      English (USA)   audio/Microsoft-wave
```

We now know the size of the file (639k or 639,000 bytes) and the exact nature of the file, a Microsoft-wave sound file. At this point, we can download the sound file to play on our computer or read or copy any of the articles.

Item number 2 above still has a right slash indicating a further menu. That path yields the following:

```
                bagpipe-archive
1.  Re: [UP] "easy" vs. "hard" re....
2.  Re: Band list (big).
3.  building an electronic bagpipe.
4.  Gordon Speirs' reedmaking paper...new info!!!.
5.  Re: [UP] "easy" vs. "hard" reeds....
6.  piping courses in Alberta?.
7.  Re: [UP] "easy" vs. "hard" re....
8.  AF Pipe Band Info.
9.  Gaita SIG.
10. Re: [UP] "easy" vs. "hard" re....
11. Re: AF Pipe Band Info.
12. Re: 9/8 Jigs, Marches.
13. Thracian gaida, etc..
14. Spanish bagpipes.
15. .BMW Tune Archive.
16. GHB for Sale.
17. Anonymous FTP site available....
18. music request.
                                      Page: 1/48
```

The sheer number of the items—forty-eight pages—and the nature of subject matter ("for sale...new info!!!") and style ("re:...piping course in Alberta?") suggest a collection of listings from a newsgroup or mailing list. (If we examine a few, we discover that this is indeed the case.)

Notice that we started our search from a computer in Minnesota (actually, from wherever we live when we called up the server) and wound up at the Dartmouth College Department of Computer Science in Hanover, New Hampshire. Other shifts in location of files are indicated with parentheses in the earlier menus.

GRAPHIC-INTERFACE PROGRAMS

We have to this point offered examples using the standard text interface program. A Gopher search with a graphic-interface program would look pretty much the same. Graphic-interface programs do, however, offer some advantages. Many of them will allow you to store a list of initial Gopher addresses as well as your personal bookmarks. They also usually contain "viewers" that enable you to hear sounds or see graphics as easily as you view texts.

Figure 10.1 illustrates a graphic-interface program for the earlier search. Here text files are indicated by eyeglasses, the sound file by musical notes, and a searchable index by an arrow over a book. Selections that shift to lower directories are indicated by an arrow to the right; return to the previous menu is indicated by an arrow to the left.

In this program, the symbol on the far left indicates whether or not the address of the particular Gopher server has been accessed. Clicking on the icon next to bagpipe-archive reveals the address and subdirectory, as indicated in the box in the middle. There *host* refers to the server computer; *selector* refers to the subdirectory on that computer.

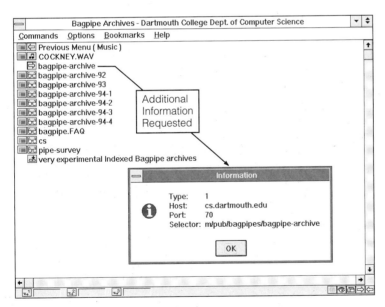

FIGURE 10.1   Gopher Menu with Site Location Indicated

FTP Versus Gopher

Gopher is essentially a browsing tool. You can pursue material on specific topics, but since you have to hunt around, it is not really a search program. Gopher is also a retrieval program. (You will recall that file transfer protocol was a retrieval program, not really a search tool, and Archie a search tool but not a tool for retrieval.)

Looking back, it should be apparent that FTP and Gopher, while both retrieval programs, serve different purposes. FTP offers a direct means of obtaining specific files. Gopher is more a tool for investigating than for locating a specific document.

The value of Gopher is in great part not only what you find at the end of your travels but what you discover along the way. The investigation itself will often suggest additional topics and resources you may never have imagined. As indicated in earlier menus, Gopher does include a direct search tool, Veronica, discussed in the next chapter.

11

Veronica

Searching with Gopher

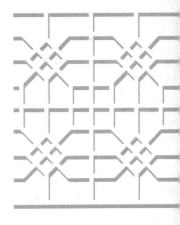

G opher is a browser. It can be described informally in hunting imagery. You start from an initial camp (an initial menu) and follow trails (menu items), ever watchful for signs of potential quarry. You slowly close in on objects of interest. If you wind up at a dead end, you can double back and try a different fork at an earlier split in the road.

Such a process is fine for hunting. Indeed, a more direct process would take the sport out of the game. But it offers a slow and laborious, as well as haphazard, approach to research.

Overview

A more direct route is available. File transfer protocol has Archie as a key-word search tool; Gopher has Veronica.

Veronica (Very Easy Rodent-Oriented Net-Wide Index to Computerized Archives) was developed at the University of Nevada at Reno in late 1992. Veronica builds a searchable index of Gopher menus in much the same way that Archie builds an index of FTP files. Every week, about a dozen Veronica sites search and index the titles in menus of more than five thousand Gopher servers. The result is a searchable index of more than fifteen million items in virtually all of the Gopher servers in the world.

Note that Veronica searches *menus,* not the *contents* of the Gopher servers themselves. Veronica indexes do, however, include additional items, such as titles from World Wide Web servers, Usenet archives, and telnet information services, that are referenced on Gopher menus.

As is the custom, we have described Veronica as Archie for Go-pherspace. But Veronica goes one step further. Archie told you where files were; you had to get them yourself using file transfer protocol. Veronica provides direct access. The output from a Veronica search is a custom Gopher menu. Veronica is truly both a search and a retrieval tool.

ACCESSING VERONICA

Since Veronica is a tool of Gophers, it appears as an option on the ini-tial menu of most Gopher servers. There is no need for a separate program, no "veronica" command. The initial Veronica menu appears as follows:

```
          Internet Gopher Information Client v1.13
    Search ALL of Gopherspace (5000+ gophers) using Veronica

 1.  How to Compose Veronica Queries - June 23, 1994.
 2.  Frequently Asked Questions (FAQ) - January 13, 1995.
 3.  More Veronica: Software,Index-Control Protocol,HTML Pages/
 4.  Simplified Veronica: Find Gopher MENUS only <?>
 5.  Simplified Veronica: Find ALL gopher types <?>
 6.  Find GOPHER DIR. by Title word(s) (UNINETT..of Bergen) <?>
 7.  Find GOPHER DIR. by Title word(s) (NYSERNet    ) <?>
 8.  Find GOPHER DIR. by Title word(s) (SUNET) <?>
 9.  Find GOPHER DIR. by Title word(s) (PSINet) <?>
10.  Find GOPHER DIR. by Title word(s) (U. Nac. Autonoma .. <?>
11.  Find GOPHER DIR. by Title word(s) (University of Koeln)<?>
12.  Search GopherSpace by Title word(s) (UNINETT of Bergen)<?>
13.  Search GopherSpace by Title word(s) (NYSERNet    ) <?>
14.  Search GopherSpace by Title word(s) (SUNET) <?>
15.  Search GopherSpace by Title word(s) (PSINet) <?>
16.  Search GopherSpace by Title word(s) (U. Nac. Autonoma. <?>
17.  Search GopherSpace by Title word(s) (U. of Koeln) <?>

Press ? for Help, q to Quit, u to go up a menu    -> Page: 1/1
```

The home Veronica is located at *gopher://veronica.scs.unr.edu.*

As with other aspects of the Internet, the relatively few Veronica indexes are often unavailable due to high traffic. During regular office hours, you might very well receive the following message:

```
        Internet Gopher Information Client v1.13
Find GOPHER DIRECTORIES by Title word(s) (via SUNET): rural 1
     *** Too many connections - Try again soon. ***.
```

Should this occur, simply try Veronica at another location.

USING VERONICA

Here, as in all research, there is a distinct art to selecting the proper search terms. Since Veronica searches for titles in menus of Gopher servers, not for the documents themselves, you might try alternate searches using synonyms or more general terms to assure yourself that you are reaching all that you might. If a search yields an inordinate number of responses, search again with a more limited search term. If you desire more options, search again with an alternative phrase or more general terms, or browse with Gopher at some of the sites indicated and see what you find.

Veronica searches are not case-sensitive (searching for *Tuba* will locate *TUBA*, *tuba*, and *Tuba*), and Veronica understands the Boolean logical operators *AND, NOT, OR* (a blank is assumed to be *AND*). Additional commands allow you to restrict the search to certain types of files or a maximum number of responses. Veronica also supports partial word searches in which an asterisk ,*, represents a "wild card" charcter or characters. **Go*** will return all items that have a word beginning with *go* in the title.

When you know exactly what term or phrase best describes what you are looking for, a Veronica search can be more direct–and potentially more fruitful–than simply following Gopher menus. In the previous chapter, we hunted for information or files on bagpipes. (Note we don't say "searched.") A Veronica search would be more direct. From a Gopher menu we access a Veronica site. The search proceeds as follows:

```
+Search GopherSpace by Title word(s) (via University of Pisa)+
¦ Words to search for bagpipe                                ¦
¦                            [Cancel ^G] [Accept - Enter]    ¦
L_____⅃

Searching Text...      Connecting...
Searching...
```

The first three pages of the outcome are presented below.

```
              Internet Gopher Information Client v1.13
Search GopherSpace by Title word(s) (via University of Pisa): bagpipe
1.  [comp.text.tex] bagpipe.tex.
2.  pipetune.zip - Play+display program/database of bagpipe tunes.
3.  [comp.text.tex] bagpipe.tex.
4.  pipetune.zip - Play+display program/database of bagpipe tunes.
5.  bagpipe-archive-92.
6.  bagpipe-archive-93.
7.  bagpipe-archive-94-1.
8.  bagpipe-archive-94-2.
9.  bagpipe-archive-94-3.
10. bagpipe-archive-94-4.
11. bagpipe.FAQ.
12. Bagpipe Archives/
13. Bagpipe Digest (fwd).
14. Bagpipe info.
15. Re: Bagpipe info.
16. Bagpipe info.
17. Re: Electronic Bagpipe Reviews....
18. Re: Bagpipe info.
Press ? for Help, q to Quit, u to go up a menu   Page: 1/7

              Internet Gopher Information Client v1.13
Search GopherSpace by Title word(s) (via University of Pisa): bagpipe
19. Electronic Bagpipe WAV file.
20. modern bagpipe music.
21. Bagpipe Society Newsletter.
22. bagpipe database.
23. Bagpipe tunes.
24. WWW Version of Bagpipe FAQ Available.
25. Developing the Swedish Bagpipe ?.
26. RE: Developing the Swedish Bagpipe ?.
27. Developing the Swedish/Any Bagpipe ?.
28. Re: Developing the Swedish/Any Bagpipe ?.
29. Re: Developing the Swedish Bagpipe ?.
30. re: Developing the Swedish/Any Bagpipe.
31. RE: Developing the Swedish Bagpipe ?.
32. RE: earliest bagpipe.
33. bagpipe info group.
34. SIGNOFF bagpipe@cs.dartmouth.edu.
```

```
35. SIGNOFF BAGPIPE@cs.dartmouth.edu.
36. Solution to noise?—bagpipe RFD.
```
```
         Internet Gopher Information Client v1.13
Search GopherSpace by Title word(s) (via University of Pisa): bagpipe
37. Re: Bagpipe Digest.
38. Re: RE: earliest bagpipe.
39. Re: RE: earliest bagpipe.
40. Re: RE: earliest bagpipe.
41. Re: RE: earliest bagpipe.
42. [GHP] Re: Small blurb on bagpipe history.
43. [GHP] Re: Small blurb on bagpipe history.
44. [GHP] Re: Small blurb on bagpipe history.
45. Re: [GHP] Re: Small blurb on bagpipe history.
46. RE: [GHP] Re: Small blurb on bagpipe history.
47. The Bagpipe Society.
48. Bagpipe list.
49. Bagpipe Making Techniques.
50. Bagpipe Making Article.
51. The Disposable Bagpipe.
52. The Disposable Bagpipe.
53. RE: The Disposable Bagpipe.
54. My essay on Bagpipe Making.
```

The listings continue for four more pages for a total of 123 items. Note that some of the items are repeated. Any difference in the address of an item on a server results in a separate listing. As this is now a Gopher menu, you can access an item by moving the cursor down and hitting enter or the right arrow.

Finally, note that the term *bagpipe* appears in every listing. This is of course as it should be. That was how the search was defined—as a search for a specific word in menu titles. But such a search will obviously fail to include a menu listing such as "pipe-survey" or the sound file "COCKNEY.WAV" that we discovered earlier using Gopher.

TEXT VERSUS GRAPHIC INTERFACE

Figure 11.1 shows the beginning of a graphic-interface Veronica search. The search produces the screen in Figure 11.2. (Turn back to

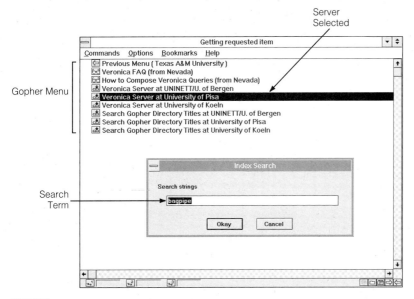

FIGURE 11.1 Selecting a Search Term (*bagpipe*) and Search Site
(*University of Pisa*) for a Veronica Search of Gopher
Menus

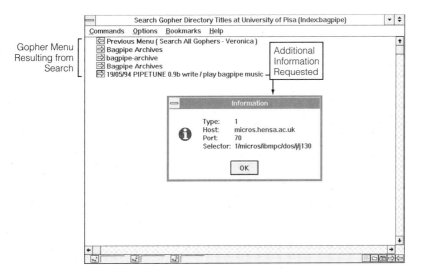

FIGURE 11.2 Gopher Menu Resulting from Veronica Search for
bagpipe at *University of Pisa*

the Gopher search to compare the results.) As indicated, the final item is from the University of Kent at Canterbury Higher Education National Software Archive (HENSA), a major archive in Great Britain.

Jughead, a variant of Veronica, is also available. Jughead (Jonzy's Universal Gopher Hierarchy Excavation and Display) produces a limited search. It looks at file names and directories on a select number of Gophers or the immediate Gopher server. As with Veronica, texts are not searched. The maximum number of entries returned is generally 1,024.

> For an extended discussion of Veronica search techniques, see the Frequently Asked Questions document at *ftp://futique.scs.unr.edu/veronica-docs/how-to-query-veronica.*

12

WAIS

Searching Documents

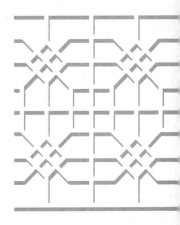

Archie searches file names in directories of anonymous FTP servers; Veronica searches key words in Gopher menus. Neither examines documents themselves, only their listing in a directory or menu. A third major approach to searching the resources of the Internet is specifically document oriented.

OVERVIEW

WAIS (Wide Area Information Servers), pronounced *waze*, was developed at Thinking Machines, Inc. and released in 1991. WAIS examines the full text of all of the documents on a particular database. It searches for key words and ranks documents according to the number and placement of the "hits." Like Veronica, WAIS offers a menu from which you can retrieve desired documents.

The WAIS search protocol on the Internet is an application of a more general protocol, and the WAIS database/document search protocol need not be over a wide area as the name implies.

In actual fact, WAIS searches not documents but *indexes* of documents. As a result, the WAIS database can include anything that can be indexed with words. Descriptions of insects or works of art can be indexed to pictures of the items. Descriptions of songs can be indexed to sound files. In the end, however, you can of course only access what has been indexed.

Examples of WAIS Databases

Aboriginal Studies (ANU)

The Book of Mormon

CancerNet (National Univ. of Singapore & National Cancer Inst.)

CIA World Factbook

Columbia University, Law Library

Department of Energy, Climate Data

Directory Cold Fusion Bibliography

Drosophila Fruitfly Stocks, Index

Early Music List and rec.music.early Archive

A Grant Getter's Guide to the Internet

Hubble Space Telescope, Instrument Status Reports,
Daily Activity

Law of the Sea

Mailing lists: the "list of lists" and Usenet newsgroups

Movie Credits/Awards Lists (from rec.arts.movies)

NASA Missions

National Institutes of Health Guide to Grants and Programs
(1991)

North American Free Trade Agreement (NAFTA)

Occupational Safety and Health Administration Act (OSHA)

Philippine Studies, 4th International Studies Conf., Abstracts

Recipes

Search the ERIC digests

Proposed U.S. Budget for 1994

Social Science Data Archives, RSSS, Australia National University

U.S. Patent Database 1994

U.S. Zipcodes

Soviet Archives

US EIA's "Petroleum Supply Monthly"

World Factbook

Zen Buddhism, Database of Dates, Anniversaries and Festivals

Using WAIS

WAIS can be accessed by the telnet command on various public-access servers, as an option on some Gopher menus, or at a site on the World Wide Web.

A WAIS search involves a number of steps:

1. Select key-word search term(s)
2. Select appropriate database(s)
3. Indicate the maximum number of responses desired
4. Search the specific database(s)
5. Refine the search as necessary
6. Access specific files

You must first decide *what* you want to find. This usually involves one or more search terms, called the *question.*

You must then decide *where* to search–that is, what documents to search. You can select from roughly six hundred free public databases, each devoted to a particular collection of materials. To search for particular song lyrics, you might try

*Sheet_Music_*Index.src at Duke University

lyrics.src at North Carolina State

bgrass-l.src at Washington and Lee University

or a database of newsgroup postings:

rec.music.early.src

In each case, notice the *src* extension indicating a database.

What if you don't know that these databases exist? The solution would be to first search a directory of servers. The directory (*directory-of-servers.scr*) at Thinking Machines (*think.com*) provides just such a starting point. Other directories are maintained by the National Science Foundation Clearinghouse for Network Information Discovery and Retrieval (CNIDR) and the Internet Network Information Center (InterNIC), another NSF-sponsored project.

Public-Access WAIS Servers	
Name	**login**
wais.wais.com	wais
quake.think.com	wais
sunsite.unc.edu	swais

In practice, a WAIS search proceeds as follows.

Assume for the moment that we wish to locate speeches in which President Clinton discussed health issues. The first step of course is to login to a WAIS server.

```
Moontower% telnet wais.wais.com
```

Upon connection, you receive the usual housekeeping information followed by a login prompt:

```
Trying 192.216.46.98...
Connected to wais.wais.com.
Escape character is '^]'.
SunOS UNIX (wais)
login:
```

Login with the appropriate command. With this location, the login command is simply **wais.** Again you receive information indicating the progress of the connection and a request for identification.

```
login: wais
Last login: Sat Aug 12 06:39:59 from mail.epsb.edmont
Welcome to swais, the text-terminal telnet client to WAIS.
Please type user identifier (optional, i.e user@host):
```

As a courtesy, type in your E-mail address and hit enter. This particular server then asks which terminal emulation you are using. Don't panic; in almost all cases you can simply hit enter to indicate the standard default of vt100.

```
TERM = (vt100) [enter key]
```

With the preliminaries accomplished, the server offers a list of WAIS databases to select from:

```
Starting up. This may take awhile...
SWAISSource Selection        Sources: 549
```

#	Server	Source	Cost
001:	[wais.access.gpo.gov]	103_cong_bills	Free
002:	[wais.access.gpo.gov]	104_cong_bills	Free
003:	[wais.access.gpo.gov]	1992_cri	Free
004:	[wais.access.gpo.gov]	1993_cri	Free
005:	[wais.access.gpo.gov]	1994_cri	Free
006:	[wais.access.gpo.gov]	1994_hob	Free

```
007:    [ wais.access.gpo.gov]    1994_record           Free
008:    [ wais.access.gpo.gov]    1994_register         Free
009:    [ wais.access.gpo.gov]    1994_unified_agenda   Free
010:    [ wais.access.gpo.gov]    1995_cri              Free
Keywords:

<space> selects, w for keywords, arrows move,
                         <return> searches, q quits, or ?
```

The list indicates the nature of the material within each database
(source) and the location of that database (server). The command
options at the bottom of the screen indicate we can select from one of
the initial list by hitting the space bar, search for a database identified
by a particular term, or simply scan through the alphabetical listing
with the arrow keys.

If we scan through the database list, we can get a sense of the
available resources along the way. But hitting the down arrow over
and over again can become tiresome. There must be some way to scan
screen by screen. If we select the help option **?**, we discover that the j
key as well as control-v (^V) and control-d (^D) all move down a
screen at a time.

Scanning through the databases, we soon discover one applicable
for our purposes.

```
 #              Server              Source            Cost
145:    [    cirm5.univ-mrs.fr]    cirm-papers         Free
146:    [      sunsite.unc.edu]    cisco-packet        Free
147:    [      sunsite.unc.edu]    clinton-speeches    Free
148:    [       zenon.inria.fr]    cm-zenon-inria-fr   Free
149:    [      biome.bio.ns.ca]    coastal             Free
150:    [      SunSite.unc.edu]    cold-fusion         Free
151:    [      com.univ-mrs.fr]    com-books           Free
152:    [      com.univ-mrs.fr]    com-papers          Free
153:    [         wais.eff.org]    comp-acad-freedom   Free
154:    [     wais.oit.unc.edu]    comp.admin          Free
155:    [     wais.oit.unc.edu]    comp.binaries       Free
Keywords:

<space> selects, w for keywords, arrows move,
                         <return> searches, q quits, or ?
```

Number 147 seems to be the desired database. We move the cursor to that line with the down arrow key and hit the space key, placing an asterisk to the left of our choice. We then type **w** to input a search term, enter the term, and hit the return (enter) key:

```
Enter keywords with spaces between them; health
                          <return> to search; ^C to cancel
```

The search begins.

```
Keywords:Searching clinton-speechess.src...
Initializing connection...
Found 40 tems. SWAIS Search ResultsItems: 40
```

```
 #     Score       Source                Title            Lines
001:   [1000]    (clinton-speeche)   HEALTH CARE: Position Pape    475
002:   [ 715]    (clinton-speeche)   HEALTH CARE: Position Pape    433
003:   [ 653]    (clinton-speeche)   THE ECONOMY: Speech - Miam    630
004:   [ 592]    (clinton-speeche)   HEALTH CARE: Speech - Litt    151
005:   [ 582]    (clinton-speeche)   HEALTH CARE: Speech - Pitt    234
006:   [ 551]    (clinton-speeche)   VARIOUS TOPICS: Interview-    830
007:   [ 459]    (clinton-speeche)   HEALTH CARE: Speech - Maco    440
008:   [ 439]    (clinton-speeche)   ECONOMIC STRATEGY: 6/21/92    877
009:   [ 429]    (clinton-speeche)   HEALTH-CARE: Position Pape    154
010:   [ 408]    (clinton-speeche)   ECONOMIC PLAN: Position Pa    773
011:   [ 377]    (clinton-speeche)   HEALTH CARE: Position Pape     93
012:   [ 367]    (clinton-speeche)   HEALTH: Speech - Philadelp    178
013:   [ 367]    (clinton-speeche)   THE ECONOMY: Statement        791
014:   [ 306]    (clinton-speeche)   VP DEBATE ANALYSIS: Encycl    697
015:   [ 296]    (clinton-speeche)   SMALL BUSINESS PLAN: Posit    598
016:   [ 275]    (clinton-speeche)   HEALTH CARE REFORM RALLY:      69
017:   [ 255]    (clinton-speeche)   THE ECONOMY: Speech - Detr    559
018:   [ 245]    (clinton-speeche)   DEMOCRATIC PARTY PLATFORM    1066
```

```
<space> selects, arrows move, w for keywords,
                          s for sources, ? for help
```

The program indicates forty selections and grades the value of each on a scale of 1 to 1,000. We have, in effect, a Gopher menu. We can select a document by moving the cursor down. In this case, select 007,

```
007:   [ 459]   (clinton-speeche)  HEALTH CARE: Speech - Maco   440
```

and access the document itself by hitting the space key.

```
Retrieving:   HEALTH CARE: Speech - Macon, GA - 9/1/92
Getting "     HEALTH CARE: Speech - Macon, GA - 9/1/92"
                                    from clinton-speech

HEALTH CARE: Speech - Macon, GA - 9/1/92

REMARKS BY GOVERNOR BILL CLINTON
MACON-GIBB SENIOR CENTER
MACON, GA
SEPTEMBER 1, 1992
```

Thank you very much. Thank you all. Thank you very
much. Mayor, I'm glad to be back in Macon, in big Biff
(phonetic) County. And this is my first trip since the
primary, so I guess I ought to thank you for your wonderful vote here in the primary.

I also want to thank those of you who asked about
Hillary. Three people said, son, if you'd just send her,
you wouldn't have to come back here any more.

I want to thank all the people who are not senior citizens who are out there beyond the ropes. I'll be out
there in just a minute; if you'll wait.

We can type **q** to return to the menu of documents and then save the
document as a file for later viewing by using an **S** "save to file" command from the listing of documents or send it to ourselves or someone
else with an **m** command. Finally, exit the WAIS program with the **q**
quit command and then exit the Internet

```
telnet> quit
Connection closed.
```

The WAIS encounter is then completed.

Figure 12.1 illustrates results of a search with a graphic-interface
WAIS Searches program.

1. The question is: health.

2. The directory of servers, *servers.src,* is to be searched.

3. A maximum listing of fifty documents has been requested. The
   search produces a listing of relevant database servers, ranked according to their probable appropriateness. (Graphic-interface programs allow you to store lists of databases. Databases discovered
   from a search can be added to your list automatically.) Here the
   third database, *USHOUSE_cong_record_104th.src,* is highlighted,
   showing that it has received a score of 147.

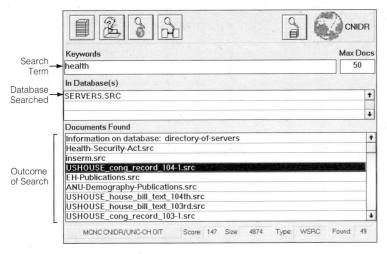

FIGURE 12.1 Menu of Servers Resulting from WAIS Search for *health* at the Directory of Servers, *SERVERS.SRC*

A search of the above database produces a list of documents ranked again according to the hits (Figure 12.2). (Note that the listings no longer end with the *.src* extension.)

As noted earlier, WAIS, like Veronica, is both a search and retrieval program. You can now retrieve a document by clicking on the item as you would with a Gopher menu.

SOME CONCERNS

WAIS searches must be executed with care. Since a single word can have different meanings in different contexts, you must decide how relevant the resulting hits actually are, and re-search if necessary. A search on the word *table,* for instance, would locate references to the physical object (kitchen table), the chart (statistical table), and the verb (table a motion). You might search on two terms that should appear equally to assure that terms appear in the proper context. Alternatively, newer WAIS programs allow for "relevance checking," a means of refining a second search based on the results of the first. Newer programs also allow the use of Boolean logic in search terms.

Above all, you must be careful not to assume that a lack of citations necessarily implies a lack of evidence. It may be that you just didn't look as imaginatively as you might.

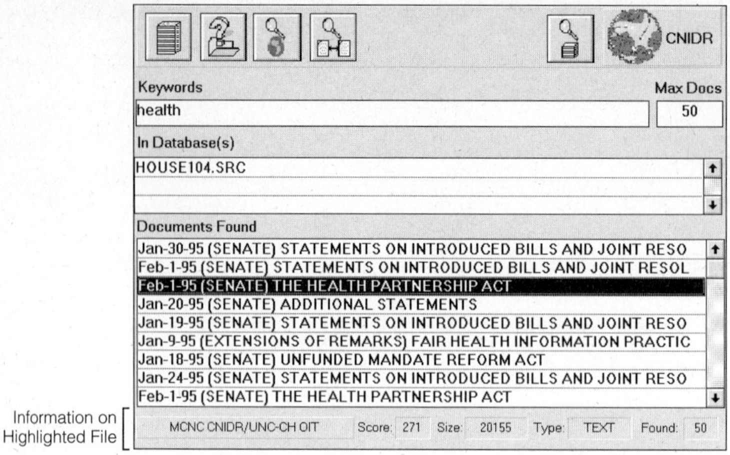

FIGURE 12.2 Menu of Documents Resulting from WAIS Search for *health* at *HOUSE104.SRC*

PERSPECTIVE

WAIS is probably the weakest link in the chain of Internet resources. The databases have been generated primarily as volunteer efforts. They exist for only a limited number of interest or topic areas. If you want to find specific terms in the President's speeches, well and good. But if you want to locate all the references to unicorns in all poems, you are out of luck. There is a database for issues of *Poetry* magazine but not for all poetry. Many WAIS indexes exist for newsgroups and professional journals; fewer exist for popular periodicals or for interest areas for which the relevant materials are widely dispersed. WAIS is suitable when you want to see where a term appears within documents or speeches. If you want to find out about the American welfare system, Gopher–or the World Wide Web–would be more appropriate.

A current listing of public-access WAIS databases is available in compressed form at *ftp://quake.think.com/pub/directory-of-servers/wais-sources.tar*. The WAIS FAQ is available from *ftp://quake.think.com/pub/wais-doc/waisfaq.txt*. WAIS searches can also be executed on the World Wide Web at *http://www.wais.com/newhomepages/default.html.*

13

The World Wide Web

The Internet as Multimedia

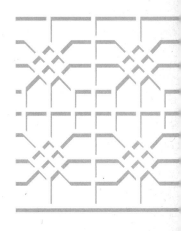

Of all the aspects of the Internet, the World Wide Web (WWW) has evoked the greatest hyperbole. Laurie Flynn, in the *New York Times*, referred to it as "an electronic amalgam of the public library, the suburban shopping mall and the Congressional Record." Peter H. Lewis, in the same newspaper, referred to it as "a time-sucking black hole . . . a speedtrap on the data highway, a Bermuda Triangle in the information ocean, the junk food aisle in cyberspace's digital supermarket."

The Web, as it's often called, was developed by the European Laboratory for Particle Physics in Geneva in 1989 as a tool for discussing research in high-energy physics. It is now the fastest growing service on the Internet. In just a few years, it has become an integral, and for some indispensable, part of the culture. It has been used by IBM to explain a takeover of Lotus when direct communication with the target company's employees was illegal, by both union and management in a Detroit newspaper strike, by Grateful Dead fans to mourn the death of Jerry Garcia, and by parents in search of a missing four-year-old.

In the three years prior to 1995, the number of Web sites grew from less than a hundred to more than ten thousand, in great part due to the release of the Mosaic browsing program in 1993. By July 1994, there were a total of eighteen thousand registered commercial *.com* addresses. Within a year, the number was up to 82,600. By the same date, the World Wide Web search program Lycos had a database of close to six million World Wide Web pages.

People are often confused as to what the term World Wide Web really refers to. It is not equivalent to the Internet itself. It is, rather, a means of obtaining information via the Internet.

As with Gopher, the World Wide Web refers to a tool for accessing files on computers connected via the Internet. The World Wide Web, then, is not a physical place, or a set of files, or even a network of computers. The heart of the World Wide Web lies in the protocols and conventions that define its use, protocols and conventions that allow access to all of the other resources of the Internet.

Two elements distinguish the Web from any other service on the Internet: the use of hypertext and the use of multimedia. We examine each of these separately, the latter first.

 ## Home Pages

Educational and cultural and governmental institutions all have World Wide Web sites:

- The White House

- A rock and roll magazine, Addicted to Noise

- A humor magazine, Melvin

- A real-time movie of a frog dissection from the University of Virginia

- A local record label, Dejadisc

- The International Federation of Red Cross and Red Crescent Societies, Geneva, Switzerland, information on federation relief operations, links to other Red Cross/Red Crescent information services, and links to other disaster-related information services

- WebChess (The Chess Server), Salem, Oregon, an experimental application that allows real-time, multiplayer chess games to be played across the Web

- The Age of Enlightenment in French painting, sponsored by the Ministère de la culture et de la francophonic, Paris, France, a panorama of 18th-century French painting

- Kesher Israel Synagogue, Washington, D.C., descriptions of synagogue activities, times of services and shabbat hospitality, hotels and restaurants in the Washington, D.C., environs

- Blacklist of Internet Advertisers, by Axel Boldt, Paderborn, NRW, Germany, a compilation of instances of offensive and inappropriate advertising on the Internet

- The Macmillan Information SuperLibrary, including audio clips from their "Politically Correct Bedtime Stories"
- New Zealand Mountain Bike Web, including lists of events, clubs, contacts, plus the full text of "Classic New Zealand Mountain Bike Rides," a guidebook that details three hundred rides nationwide

---

THE LOOK!

The World Wide Web is the only truly multimedia presentation on the Internet.

Gopher menus can lead to files that contain pictures or sound or even movie clips. You can save these files and with a proper viewer "open" them like any other. But the overall presentation of the menus is text. Graphics and sound are not integrated with the menu screens.

You have only to look at a World Wide Web screen to see the difference! Each Web site starts from an initial menu or home page—what Michael Neubarth, editor-in-chief of *Internet World,* has called "a combination frontispiece, greeting room, table of contents, hub, and launching pad." Figure 13.1 is the opening screen of the home page of the Congressional Web site, Thomas (named for Thomas Jefferson and/or The House Open Multimedia Access System).

Web screens typically display a number of typefaces and icons. Photographs and drawings are integrated with the text material. Sound files can be played by clicking on an icon. Recent increases in computer speed as well as faster sound and video boards have spawned applications utilizing real-time sound and 3-D or virtual reality graphics.

To be sure, the World Wide Web can be accessed with a text interface, but it has none of the panache of the graphics version. Elements that would appear highlighted by color in a graphic interface appear as underlined or shadowed text. Figure 13.2 is a text-based version of the earlier screen.

Clearly, text-interface displays are a significant compromise.

WHAT'S BEHIND IT ALL: HYPERTEXT

The World Wide Web is based on the notion of hypertext. In a hypertext document, key concepts and ideas are coded with the address of related material—in much the same manner as each item in a Gopher

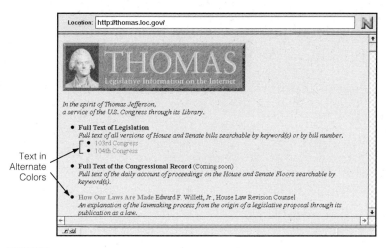

FIGURE 13.1 Thomas World Wide Web Home Page with Graphics

Text in
Alternate
Colors

```
THOMAS: Legislative Information on the Internet (p1
of 4) [Thomas Jefferson logo]
In the spirit of Thomas Jefferson,
a service of the U.S. Congress through its Library.

* Full Text of Legislation

Full text of all versions of House and Senate bills
searchable by keyword(s) or by bill number.

+  103rd Congress
+  104th Congress

* Full Text of the Congressional Record (Coming soon)

Full text of the daily account of proceedings on the
House and Senate Floors searchable by keyword(s).

*  How Our Laws Are Made    Edward F. Willett, Jr.,
                            House Law Revision Counsel
```

FIGURE 13.2 Text-Based Version of Thomas Home Page

menu is encoded. The highlighted terms and icons in the examples above indicate such links. Click on them, and you're sent to a "linked" Web page–again, much as you might move from item to item in a Gopher menu.

The coding of the links in a World Wide Web document is done with Hypertext Markup Language (HTML). A Web browser is in reality an HTML reader.

The following is the HTML document underlying the opening screen for Thomas viewed earlier. Addresses are indicated in universal resource locator (URL) notation (see Chapter 4). On-screen text has been marked in boldface to distinguish it from the hypertext markup language coding.

<!doctype html public "-//W30//DTD WWW HTML 2.0//EN">
<HTML>
<HEAD>
<TITLE>**THOMAS: Legislative Information on the Internet**</TITLE>
<!BASE HREF="http://thomas.loc.gov/home/thomas.html">
</HEAD>
<BODY>
<img src= "http://thomas.loc.gov/home/thom_mas.gif" alt="[**Thomas Jefferson logo**] ">
<P><EM>**In the spirit of Thomas Jefferson,**
a service of the U.S. Congress through its Library.</EM>
<UL>
<P>
<LI><STRONG>**Full Text of Legislation**</STRONG>

<EM>**Full text of all versions of House and Senate bills searchable by keyword(s) or by bill number.**</EM>
<UL>
<LI><a href="http://thomas.loc.gov/home/c103query.html">**103rd Congress**</a>
<LI><a href="http://thomas.loc.gov/home/c104query.html">**104th Congress**</a>
</UL>
<P>
<LI><STRONG>**Full Text of the Congressional Record**</STRONG> **(Coming soon)**

<EM>**Full text of the daily account of proceedings on the House and Senate Floors searchable by keyword(s).**</EM>

```
<P>
<LI><a
href="http://thomas.loc.gov/home/lawsmade.toc.html"><STRONG>How
```
Our Laws Are Made</STRONG></a> **Edward F. Willett, Jr.,
House Law
Revision Counsel**
```
<BR><EM>
```
**An explanation of the lawmaking process from the
origin of a legislative proposal through its publication as a
law.**</EM>

....

....

The universal resource location notation *http://* refers to Hypertext
Transfer Protocol, the main operating system of the World Wide Web.
This protocol instructs your computer to connect to the computer at
the specified address, request the specified document, receive the document, and finally sever the connection.

As described so far, the Web works much like Gopher menus.
However, it goes further. The links are not limited to menu lines. Hypertext links can be inserted into maps or drawings. You can click on a
room in a blueprint and see a photograph of that room. Hypertext
allows for links anywhere within a paragraph. Footnote numbers can
provide direct access to the original sources.

Pundits thus delight in stressing that hypertext is nonlinear. Reading a hypertext document, you do not need to follow a predetermined
sequence of ideas. You can branch off as your interests dictate. It is as
though you were reading an encyclopedia and with a snap of your
fingers can instantly shift to another page, another book, or even a
phonograph or slide projector! In the classic example often used to
describe a similar process with CD-ROM disks, a child can read about
the moon, click on the term *exploration* to jump to a discussion of the
first lunar landing, and click on a picture of Neil Armstrong to hear
the words "There's one small step for a man … one giant leap for
mankind …"

The Hypertext Language

*A primer on hypertext vocabulary and syntax is available
at http://www.ncsa.uiuc.edu/General/Internet/WWW/
HTMLPrimer.html*

ACCESSING THE WORLD WIDE WEB

The World Wide Web is accessible with programs called browsers, such as the now-famous graphic-interface Mosaic. Text-based browsers such as Lynx can be launched from public-access sites using the telnet command or as selections on the higher-level menus of many Gophers. Alternatively, access with Lynx is available directly from a provider prompt. Simply type **lynx** followed by a Web address expressed in URL format:

`Moontower%`**lynx http://thomas.loc.gov**

The command **lynx** alone accesses the default home page of your Internet provider.

Graphic-interface programs such as Mosaic or Netscape follow essentially the same process. Simply enter an appropriate address (or use the default site) and click on highlighted terms or icons to move from site to site. No fancy commands are necessary. A chimp can do it!

USING THE WORLD WIDE WEB

World Wide Web browsers allow you to access Web locations, follow hypertext links, return to previous locations, and create both book-marks and an ongoing history of the sites visited in your travels.

World Wide Web FAQ

The World Wide Web FAQ, offering discussion of both World Wide Web resources and browsers, is located at *http://sunsite.unc.edu/boutell/faq/www_faq.html*

You can keep up with the ever-expanding list of home pages by checking the newsgroup *alt.Internet.services* or by subscribing to net-happenings-digest from *majordomo@is.internic.net* with the message "subscribe net-happenings-digest".

As with all menus, you have to start somewhere. A number of options exist. You can use the opening (default) home page accessed by your browser. If you have a "yellow pages" of addresses or have written an address down, you can go directly to a specific site. If you have used that browser before, you will have saved a list of bookmarks leading to your favorite sites. Alternatively, you can start from one of a number of indexes or a key-word search. These and other resources are discussed in Chapter 16, "Internet Resources for Research."

THE GLORY AND THE HYPE

The attention given the World Wide Web is in huge part deserved–but only in part.

Due to the added space required by fancy fonts and graphics, the "text" of most hypertext displays on the World Wide Web is decidedly cursory. The full opportunity for lengthy discussion is rarely taken; you are instead left with an illustrated and annotated menu, as with the earlier Thomas home page. In addition, whereas a Gopher menu might offer fifteen possible paths on a single screen, the opening screen of a Web site usually has no more than five links, if that many. While many Gopher menus are complete on a single screen, a full view of most Web pages requires scanning a number of screens. These problems are clearly due in part to a lack of sophistication in writing Web pages, but the problems remain.

Content is also an issue. Many corporate home pages have been compared to the electronic equivalent of junk mail, filled with "turgid company profiles, hokey product pitches and bland marketing material…that wouldn't make it from the mailbox to the kitchen counter of most homes if they arrived via the Postal Service."*

Speed is another consideration. You pay for graphics with reduced speed. In the earlier example of the Web site Thomas, the text version of the opening page requires 3,365 bytes of information. The full graphics version uses 31,517 bytes. In short, the screen with full graphics takes ten times as long to receive and display. With a 14,400-baud modem, the wait is annoying and at times seems interminable–and

*Bart Zeigler, "In Cyberspace the Web Delivers Junk Mail," *Wall Street Journal*, June 13, 1995, pp. B1, B6.

that's not to mention the delay with animation, sound messages, or movies! In response to this problem, new browsers load the text first, painting in pictures later, or allow you to view the screen in a text format with pictures replaced by icons, as in Figure 13.3.

Finally, just as anyone can establish a bulletin board, so anyone on the Internet can establish a home page presence on the Web. There is no committee to go through, no certification to acquire, no large investment in hardware required. Many Internet providers and on-line services now offer this opportunity to their subscribers.

The ease with which Web sites can be established has both advantages and disadvantages. On the one hand, it guarantees openness and diversity. On the other hand, the Web is subject to an overabundance of choices, many of questionable value. With broader access to the Web via on-line services, the increase in new sites has been accelerated by businesses anticipating methods for secure credit card transactions on the Internet.

Even with all the problems, in many instances the resources of the Web are without equal. For maps, product pictures, photographs, art work, and other illustrative material, there is no substitute.

Browsing the Web may best be compared to rummaging through the world's academic, governmental, commercial, and entertainment attics, an ever increasing wealth of information on the arts, business, politics, and daily living, as evident from the gallery of World Wide Web home pages that follows this chapter (Figures 13.4–13.11).

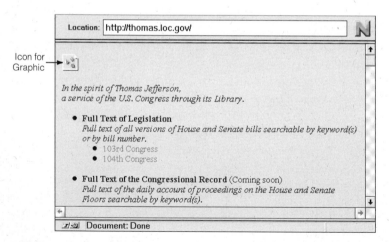

FIGURE 13.3   Thomas World Wide Web Home Page without Graphics

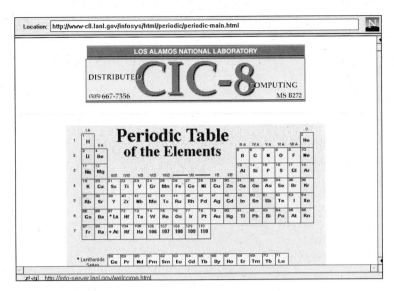

FIGURE 13.4   Los Alamos Periodic Table Site

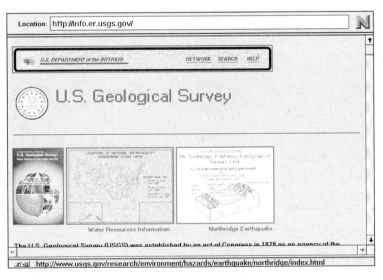

FIGURE 13.5   United States Geological Survey

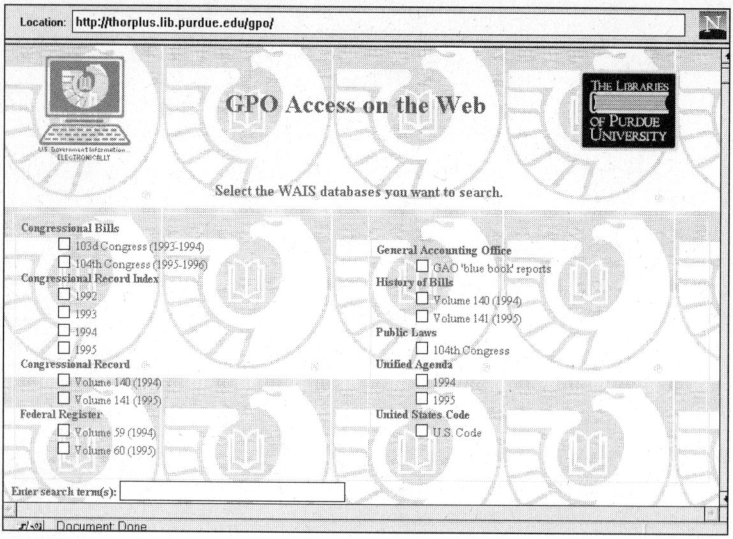

FIGURE 13.6   United States Government General Printing Office

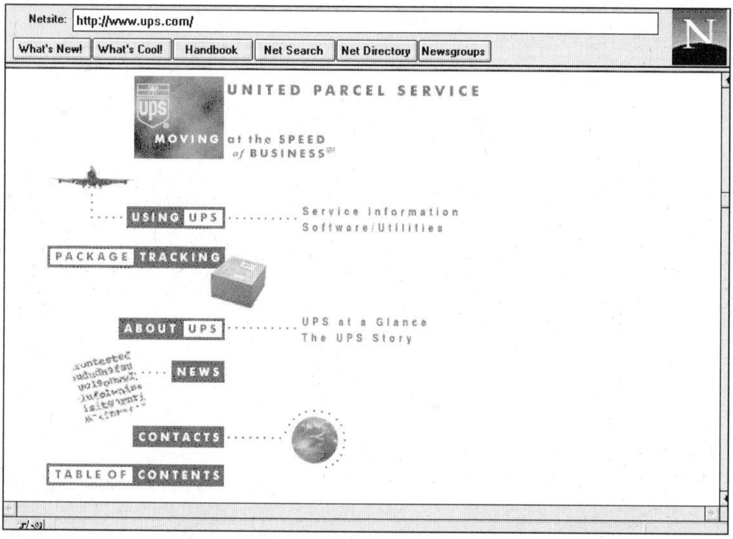

FIGURE 13.7   United Parcel Service

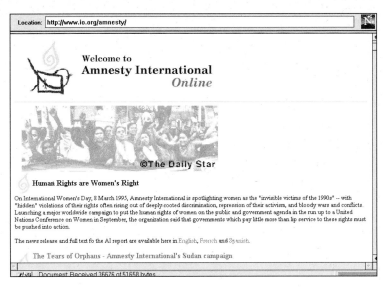

FIGURE 13.8   Amnesty International

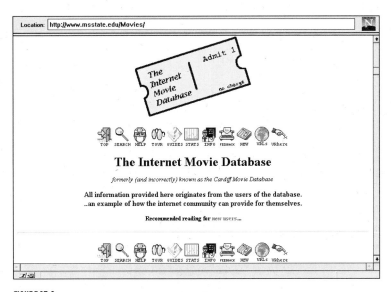

FIGURE 13.9   The Internet Movie Database

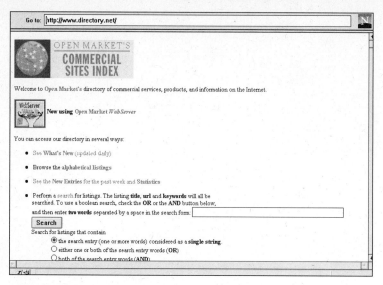

FIGURE 13.10   Open Market's Commercial Sites Index

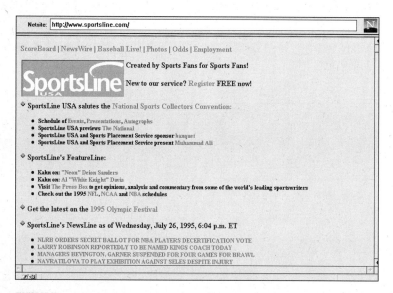

FIGURE 13.11   SportsLine

Doing Research on the Internet

General Concerns

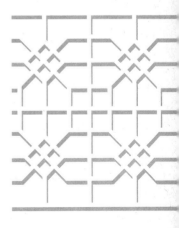

W hat am I looking for, and where can I find it? Research is (1) initiated by questions, (2) guided by knowledge and reflection, and (3) driven by feedback–all of which is to say that much of research is a matter of trial and error. But it is a methodical and informed trial and error.

Research Is Initiated by Questions

Research begins with questions, with wanting to know something. There are the traditional questions of news reporters: *who* did *what, where, when,* and *why?* Questions may address facts that everyone accepts or diverse views on an issue. You may seek specific information about a specific topic (what is the atomic weight of uranium?) or a wide range of ideas on a broad topic (what causes global warming?). One way or another, you want to know something you don't already know.

If you think you know it all, there is no need for research. If you want to check your knowledge or understanding, that is in itself a question: Am I right? That is a legitimate basis for research.

Finally, research assumes that the information you want to know exists, that it is accessible, and that you can find it. The real question then is where to look or–even more to the point–how to find out where to look. Which brings us to the second point.

RESEARCH IS GUIDED BY KNOWLEDGE AND REFLECTION

The more you know about what you want to find, the easier it is to find it. This may seem obvious, but it is also profound. Without prior reflection, you can waste hours chasing inappropriate sources, hours that could be saved with a little thought before you started.

Different kinds of information will obviously be found in different places. Without knowing *something* about what you are looking for, you cannot even start! Where, for instance, should you look for information on the origin of the capo? (The hope here is that you have never heard of a capo. If you have, substitute carbonaceous chondrites.) A dictionary, you say. But the word does not appear in many dictionaries. Then in what context did the term appear? Surely that will provide a start. Alternatively, you might ask, who cares? Not who gives a damn, but who would want to know? If you know who cares about a topic or an issue, you are well along the way to finding out who might collect information, store it, and have it available.

But what about the capo? The notion of origins suggests historical development. If you know that guitarists use capos, life is obviously easier. You could approach the topic in terms of guitars, the playing of stringed instruments, or the history of musical instruments. (A capo is a device for changing the tuning of a guitar.) Here, as elsewhere, research requires that you generalize, that you recognize the *kind* of thing you are dealing with, that you classify or categorize ideas. Once you recognize the kind of information you are seeking, you are well on your way to realizing where it might be found.

Text Resources

Knowing where to look depends greatly on knowing where you *might* look. Library research draws on a variety of text resources. You might use the card catalog and a microfiche or microfilm reader. Common sources include encyclopedias, bibliographies, concordances, thesauruses, dictionaries, telephone books, gazetteers, atlases, newspaper and periodical indexes, handbooks, fact books, almanacs, and other compilations of useful information.

You must also be aware of the existence and uses of standard resources in your specific field of interest, whether it be astronomy or astrology, canning or canoeing. Chemists have to know about the *Handbook of Chemistry and Physics*, musicians about *Grove's Music Encyclopedia*.

Electronic Resources

Just as there are traditional archives of paper resources, there are also archives of electronic resources.

You should be aware of the following electronic resources—again, both in general and in your field of interest:

databases (both public and commercial)

specialized on-line library collections

Gopher and Web servers of professional associations, government agencies, and nonprofit organizations

Usenet newsgroups and frequently asked questions

discussion groups and newsgroups

anonymous ftp software archives

Students, faculty, and many businesspeople often have access to commercial databases such as Nexis/Lexis or Dialog, whether on-line or on CD-ROM in libraries.

RESEARCH IS DRIVEN BY FEEDBACK

Research is a matter of discovery, discrimination, and elimination. When you look for information, you either find what you want—or you don't. If you do, well and good. If you don't, the trick is to turn momentary failure into a productive learning experience: the discovery of the *absence* of data is often as important as discovery of relevant data itself. Is nothing there, or did you just not find it? If not here, then where? Try alternate search strategies to assure that information is truly unavailable. As you search, you will discover new interests or topics. As you eliminate one source, you will be led to others. Everything you find or do not find shapes your further inquiry.

OTHER FACTORS

Research, especially scholarly or academic research, is driven by a number of other factors. These factors include identifying the authorship of remarks, evaluating the authority of remarks, and authenticating the source and/or origin of remarks. As we shall see in the next chapter, these issues can be called into question when engaging in research on the Internet.

15

Internet Concerns

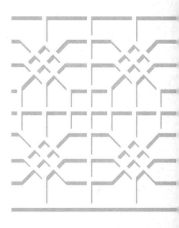

You may turn to the Internet to save time, to save effort, or to find better sources of information. But just because you have access to the Internet does not mean the Internet is necessarily the best tool for finding the information you want. Many times, other procedures are quicker, easier, or more reliable.

TRY THE OBVIOUS FIRST

The general rule is, try the obvious first. This seems self-evident, but it often needs restating. To find the location of Pisa, Italy, you can turn on your computer, access your Internet service, call up a browser program, look up the address of an appropriate site, connect to that site, search for *Pisa*, and wait for a response. Alternatively, you can flip to the back of most dictionaries and look it up in the pronouncing gazetteer. There's a lesson there.

In the discussion of Gophers in Chapter 10, we searched for information on bagpipes. Had we wanted a definition of bagpipes, we would have done better looking in a dictionary, whether on-line or not. Had we wanted to know the history of bagpipes, we would have done better simply looking in a general or specialized encyclopedia in the library. In similar fashion, Project Gutenberg has a thesaurus available on-line, but you may also have a thesaurus built into your word processor or a copy of one on your shelf.

Selecting Internet Resources

The Internet contains various resources. Each is useful for different purposes. Which you turn to will depend on what you are looking for:

E-mail–to communicate with specific people

Listserv–for contact with individuals as representatives of an organization or having a specific interest

Newsgroups–for current discussion of a particular topic or issue

FTP–to acquire specific computer files. If you are not sure where to find files, the associated search program, Archie, is a useful tool

Gopher–to locate documents, files, information, data, or personal contacts from or about a specific educational, governmental, or nonprofit organization or association. The associated search program, Veronica, provides tailor-made Gopher menus

WAIS–for full-text searches of documents

World Wide Web–to locate documents, files, information, or data from or about a specific business or commercial enterprise, especially for product information and technical assistance. Also appropriate for entertainment, hobby, and cultural phenomena. And the Web is the choice for most multimedia presentations, whether sound, movies, or simple graphics

Finally, remember that many World Wide Web browsers can provide direct links to other aspects of the Internet.

Networking for Knowledge

The car manufacturer Packard long ago had a slogan: Ask the man who owns one. With research: Ask someone who knows. If you know whom to ask, send an E-mail message to that person. If you do not know his or her E-mail address, you can use a variety of search programs for finding E-mail addresses, but the best way is still to use the telephone to call and ask someone. (Short of that, it is easier to find E-mail addresses on local network indexes than on wider databases.)

If you do not know whom to ask, check recent newsgroup postings, archives of newsgroup frequently asked questions, or the postings of a relevant discussion group for names and E-mail addresses. Check the rosters of governmental, academic, or nonprofit organizations. But do your homework first. Know exactly what it is you want to know, and do not bother others when a little time in the library would do the trick.

In the end, you are more likely to gain new insights and understanding through the interchange of talking to someone else than you are punching keys on a keyboard and staring at a computer screen.

ORDER AND ORGANIZATION

Reflect for a moment on how you engage in research without the Internet. You would, first of all, go where you would expect the information to be. You would check spelling in a dictionary or investigate the Battle of Gettysburg in a Civil War history book. You would not walk to a shelf in the library and start sifting through books for an appropriate source. Books are, after all, placed on the shelves in some distinct order; they are cataloged according to what they have in them.

While there is no catalog of all of the books in all of the libraries in the world, there *are* search programs for all of the Internet servers in the world. These search programs are efficient, but they may not be comprehensive or discriminating in the choice of leads that they offer. The problem of assessing the usefulness or quality of information remains. While we may delight in the fact that we can post anything we want on sections of the Internet, when we are looking for information on the Battle of Gettysburg we would like to be able to distinguish beforehand between a professor's treatise and Jonny's seventh-grade school report. Which brings us to the next area of concern.

> Picture yourself trying to find the bathroom in a house with 25,000 unmarked doors.
> From an advertisement for the magazine *Internet Voyager*

ASSUMPTIONS OF AUTHENTICITY

On the whole, Internet data is no more authoritative than any other—and in many cases less so.

Return to the earlier image of library research. When you examine a book or professional journal on the shelf, you are aware that it has been selected from among competing texts by an editor for publication and chosen from among competing publications by a librarian for inclusion in the collection. The title page and copyright page attest to the true author and the place and date of publication. And you can be reasonably certain the manuscript exists in the form intended by the author.

With the Internet, all of these assumptions may fall under suspicion. Much that is on the internet is "unsigned," as it were—you have no idea who wrote it. When it is easy to invent personae, it is hard to verify credentials. The affiliation of a server may suggest a certain degree of reliability but in itself indicates neither approval nor review by anyone else at that institution.

We might consider a hierarchy of trustworthiness for different aspects of the Internet. We might give greatest credence to material appearing on a Gopher, since setting up a Gopher requires the expense of establishing a server computer. Institutions and corporations, not individuals, generally set up Gopher sites. In this scenario, the weakest link might be Usenet newsgroups, since in many cases anyone can post anything without any review or approval. Such a scenario might be comforting, but it is also specious, since in many instances material based on one source can be accessed from another without our being aware of it.

Finally, since it is easier to publish material on the Internet than it is to publish books, information available on the Internet is often more up to date than information in printed texts. But not all information

> ### Getting Help
> For useful guidelines on the appropriate use of newsgroups and discussion groups as sources for research, see "The art of getting help" from *The Network Observer*, Volume 1, Number 2 (*http://ccc.wustl.edu/~cs142/articles/MISC/art_of_getting_help-agre*)

changes frequently or has changed recently. A listing of the highest mountains might be found more quickly in a handbook.

BUDGETING TIME

The general rule for efficient use of the Internet is simple: logon, get what you want, and logoff. You want to know what you're looking for beforehand and have a plan for accessing it. This is especially true when you are incurring hourly expenses imposed by on-line services or Internet providers.

You can save time and money by downloading information for later perusal. Off-line time is cheaper than on-line time, and hard copies (that is, paper texts) are easier to read than text on screens. Both text and graphic-interface programs offer automatic capture of on-screen text during a session. You can save any hypertext pages you view on the World Wide Web for closer examination off-line.

Spend your time on-line evaluating information, not looking up addresses. If your software program allows it, maintain your own directories of useful sites for FTP, Gopher, and WAIS programs. If this is not possible, keep a log of addresses handy. When using Gopher and World Wide Web programs, make bookmarks for sites you return to often.

CITATIONS AND PLAGIARISM

You can save time and effort by downloading documents instead of finding published texts and photocopying them. You can then retrieve these files directly into your own writing with a word processor. While convenient, this process has obvious dangers. You can confuse your text with text that you have downloaded and in so doing commit the crime of plagiarism. You can also lose track of information for proper citations. (The Internet address of documents is often equivalent to the publication data associated with books.)

You can avoid plagiarism a number of ways. To distinguish between your work and that of others, retrieve text into your document in a specific font, such as italicized. (On screen, any color change will do.) When you have properly quoted or paraphrased and footnoted remarks, then and only then eliminate the italics. When your text is complete, go back and delete any remaining italicized sections.

Alternatively, word processing programs often allow you to insert comments within a discussion. These boxed remarks appear on screen but do not print. Place source material and citations in these comment boxes. Like this:

New York Times, **April 23, 1995, p. 23.**

Once you have properly quoted or paraphrased the material, convert the citation information in the comment box into a footnote.

Finally, even when the Internet is the best source, you only save time if you are familiar with the appropriate resources and know how to access them. That means such things as knowing the addresses of subject menus and why you might choose to use Veronica instead of a World Wide Web search program. It means knowing whether a particular search program accepts Boolean logic in its search terms and how to properly formulate searches. Which brings us to the next chapter.

16

Internet Resources for Research

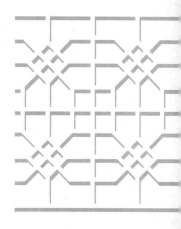

With research, as with all things, you have to start somewhere. You have to assess your current knowledge and decide what you want to know. You also have to select the tools with which to work.

Library research might begin with the card catalog and a general reference work such as a bibliography or encyclopedia. The Internet offers two approaches to research: browsing and searching. Browsing involves making choices from possible options as you move from one source to another. Searching is more straightforward: you tell a search engine what to find, and it goes out and examines various databases for you. Gopher menus and World Wide Web links offer choices for browsing. Archie, Veronica, and WAIS, as well as various World Wide Web search programs, offer key-word search programs.

Although obviously more direct, searching can be hit and miss. If you do not carefully choose your search term, your search program, and the database to be searched, the search can fail not because resources do not exist but because the search program simply did not find them. Browsing may often appear random or haphazard, but it does offer continuous opportunities to refocus an investigation according to the available resources.

> The next best thing to knowing something is knowing where to find it.
> Samuel Johnson
>
> Everything you need to know is on the Internet. You just can't find it.
> Anonymous

DESK REFERENCE TOOLS

We might start with electronic versions of standard library resources. Many universities offer access to basic desk reference tools on World Wide Web or Gopher menus. Desk reference tools typically include items such as the following:

U.S. Geographic Names Database

U.S. Telephone Area Codes

Webster's Dictionary

CIA World Factbook 1991

Associated Press/Reuters News Wire Service

Since encyclopedias are expensive, they are generally not available free. Desk reference tools can be accessed at the following sites:

University of Maryland
http://www.umbc.edu/reference-info.html

Indiana State
gopher://odin.indstate.edu:70/11/ref.dir/info.dir

National Institutes of Health
gopher://gopher.niaid.nih.gov

University of Michigan
http://www.sils.umich.edu/~nscherer/RefDesk.html

As the example that follows suggests, desk reference tool menus can offer a useful starting point for many areas of research.

The Virtual Reference Desk at Purdue University

(http://thorplus.lib.purdue.edu/reference/index.html)

This desk reference includes the following:

Dictionaries, Thesaurus, Acronyms

Search Webster's Dictionary (from Carnegie-Mellon University)

Search the American English Dictionary (from the National Institutes of Health)

Search English and Technical Dictionary (from CERN)

Dictionary Search (from Bucknell)

College Slang Dictionary (from Spies.com)

French-English dictionary (from ARTFL)

German-English Dictionary (from Darmstadt, Germany)

Japanese-English dictionary (by jfriedl)

English-Slovene and Slovene-English dictionary (from Slovenia)

Search the Free On-Line Dictionary of Computing (from the United Kingdom)

Search the Hacker's Dictionary/Jargon File (from Austria)

Search Acronym Dictionary (from Ireland)

Search an Acronym Dictionary (from the United Kingdom site 1)

Search an Acronym Dictionary (from the United Kingdom site 2)

Search an updated 1911 Roget's Thesaurus (from the National Institutes of Health)

Browse the NASA Thesaurus (from NASA)

See also the human languages page at Willamette

Bartlett's Book of Familiar Quotations

Maps & Travel Information

1991 World Factbook-CIA edition (from the University of Minnesota)

1993 CIA World Factbook (from San Francisco State University)

CIA World Factbooks / 1992 - present (from University of Missouri-St. Louis)

Latest Edition of the World Factbook (from University of Missouri-St. Louis)

Country Studies (from the Library of Congress)

Map Collection (from the University of Texas, Austin)

Map Viewer (from Xerox Palo Alto Research Center)

Geographic database (from MIT)

U.S. Gazetteer (from SUNY at Buffalo)

Canadian Geographical Names (The National Atlas Information Service [Canada])

U.S. State Department Travel Advisories (Browse) (from the University of Pennsylvania)

U.S. State Department Travel Advisories (Search) (from St. Olaf College)

Koblas Currency Converter (from O'Reilly and Associates, Inc.)

Selected U.S. Documents

White House Home Page (also gateway to Executive Agencies)

U.S. House of Representatives (direct from the House of Representatives)

U.S. Supreme Court Decisions (made available by the Cornell University Legal Information Institute)

Federal Register Table of Contents

Thomas, a project of the Library of Congress, provides a searchable index to the Congressional Record on a daily basis. It also includes the full text of all bills that have been submitted to the current session of Congress.

Historical Documents (from the Queens Library NYC)

Declaration of Independence (from the Queens Library NYC)

U.S. Constitution (from the Queens Library NYC)

U.S. Budget (1995) (from the University of North Carolina)

White House File (from Carnegie-Mellon University)

1990 Census data (from the University of Michigan)

U.S. Census server (from the Bureau of the Census)

1980 & 1990 U.S. Census (from Lawrence Berkeley Labs)

Internal Revenue Service (from the Department of the Treasury)

Periodic Tables and Weights & Measures

Weights & Measures (from the University of Oregon)

Periodic Table 1 (from the University of California at Berkeley)

Periodic Table 2 (from the University of Kansas)

Periodic Table 3 (from Spies.com)

Phone Books & Area Codes

Purdue Student & Staff Directory (from the Purdue University Computing Center)

Selected phone books for North American institutions (from the University of Notre Dame)

University White Pages (from the University of Illinois)

Airline 800 Telephone Numbers (from Princeton University)

Telecom Digest Guide to Area Codes (from MIT)

Search for Area Codes (from Bucknell)

AT&T 800 Number Directory

World Wide Yellow Pages

General Gopher to X.500 Gateway (University of Michigan)

ZIP & International Country Codes

U.S. Postal Service ZIP+4 Lookup (from the U.S. Postal Service)

Zip Codes for U.S. Cities (from the University of Oregon)

U.S.A. Zip Codes (from the University of Minnesota)

The National Address Server (from the University of Buffalo)

U.S. Gazetteer (from the University of Buffalo)

U.S. Postal Service Abbreviations (from Princeton University)

Internet Country Codes (from the University of California at Irvine)

Time & Date

Date and Time Gateway (from Berkeley Software Design, Inc.)

Time Around the World (from the Cleveland Public Library)

Calendar–Search (from New Mexico State University)

Calendar–Month (from the U.S. Navy)

Calendar–Year (from the University of Utah)

Other Reference Sources

Selected Dissertations (from University Microfilms International)

Vanderbilt News Archive (from Vanderbilt University)

South Bend Tribune Index (from the St. Joseph County Public Library)

Index to Metro section, with abstracts, since 1990

1994 Indiana State Legislators (from the St. Joseph County Public Library)

Detailed information, including a picture, of each Indiana State Senator and Representative

Online Reference Works (from Carnegie-Mellon University)

UCSC Reference (from the University of California at Santa Cruz)

UCSD Reference Shelf (from the University of California at San Diego)

NOVA Reference Shelf (from Nova Southeastern University)

SUBJECT GUIDES

Library books are organized according to subject matter, whether as novels, biographies, or under the headings of nonfictional works (history, astronomy, sociology, and so forth). Academic study is divided into disciplines in similar fashion. Divisions such as these can, at times, fragment research in artificial ways. Should homelessness be studied in terms of economics, sociology, anthropology, or city planning? On one hand, it all depends on your emphasis or perspective; on the other, all approaches are appropriate. Subject classification has, however, proven to be one of the more useful ways of organizing information, and the Internet contains a number of superb subject indexes.

One of the most comprehensive subject indexes is offered by the National Center for Supercomputing Applications (NCSA) at the University of Illinois at Urbana-Champaign. It is properly entitled the Internet Resources Meta-Index (*http://ncsa.uiuc.edu/ncsameta.html*). Other useful subject indexes include the following:

Gopher Jewels
Available on most Gopher menus.

Special Internet Connections, by Scott Yanoff
http://www.uwm.edu/Mirror/inet.services.html

WWW Virtual Library (CERN) (Figure 16.1)
http://www.w3.org/hypertext/DataSources/bySubject/Overview.html

YAHOO (Yet Another Hierarchically Odiferous Oracle)
http://www.yahoo.com

Whole Internet Catalog
http://nearnet.gnn.com/gnn/wic/index.html

EINet Galaxy
http://www.einet.net/galaxy.html

Carnegie-Mellon Humanities Gopher
gopher://english-server.hss.cmu.edu

Solinet (Southeastern Library Network)
gopher://sol1.solinet.net

The Educational Resources on the Internet Guide/Magpie
http://www.dcs.aber.ac.uk/~jjw0/index_ht.html

FedWorld
http://www.fedworld.gov

Government Information Locator Service (GILS)
http://info.er.usgs.gov/gils/index.html

Library of Congress (MARVEL–Machine-Assisted Realization of the Virtual Electronic Library)
gopher://marvel.loc.gov

Open Market's Commercial Sites Index
http://www.directory.net

World Wide Web Yellow Pages
http://www.yellow.com

The best resource list of course is the one *you* develop from your own experience to meet your own needs. Gopher and Web programs allow you to store the address of useful sites for later recall in a "bookmark" or "hot list" (the name varies with the browser used). Graphic-interface FTP programs also allow you to store addresses of useful sites for later recall.

DISCIPLINE-SPECIFIC GUIDES

Every discipline has specialized resources. The Clearinghouse for Subject-Oriented Internet Resource Guides, jointly sponsored by the University of Michigan and Argus Associates, offers guides to resources on the Internet for more than three hundred subject areas, from statistics to women's health resources, job hunting to alternative medicine (*ftp://archive.umich.edu/inetdirs*). A Gopher version (*gopher://gopher.lib.umich.edu*) and a hypertext version are also available (*http://www.lib.umich.edu/chhome.html*). The guides often run twenty to thirty pages.

Three other subject-oriented listings, all updated regularly, are also deserving of special mention:

- **The SURAnet Guide to Selected Internet Resources**
  ftp://ftp.sura.net/pub/nic/infoguide.<month>-<year>.txt.

- **Information Sources: the Internet and Computer-Mediated Communication,** by John December
  ftp://ftp.rpi.edu/pub/communications/Internet-tools

- **Special Internet Connections,** by Scott Yanoff
  ftp://csd4.csd.uwm.edu/pub/inet.services.txt.

The final site also exist as World Wide Web menus, as indicated earlier. Guides such as these can be invaluable sources of addresses for further investigation.

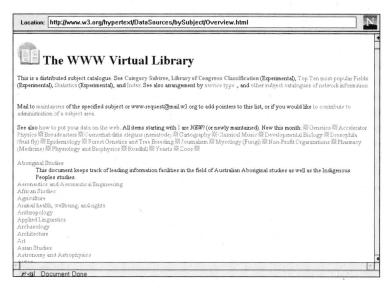

Location: http://www.w3.org/hypertext/DataSources/bySubject/Overview.html

The WWW Virtual Library

This is a distributed subject catalogue. See Category Subtree, Library of Congress Classification (Experimental), Top Ten most popular Fields (Experimental), Statistics (Experimental), and Index. See also arrangement by service type , and other subject catalogues of network information

Mail to maintainers of the specified subject or www-request@mail.w3.org to add pointers to this list, or if you would like to contribute to administration of a subject area.

See also how to put your data on the web. All items starting with ! are *NEW!* (or newly maintained). New this month: Genetics Accelerator Physics Broadcasters Caenorhabditis elegans (nematode) Cartography Classical Music Developmental Biology Drosophila (fruit fly) Epidemiology Forest Genetics and Tree Breeding Journalism Mycology (Fungi) Non-Profit Organizations Pharmacy (Medicine) Physiology and Biophysics Roadkill Yeasts Zoos

Aboriginal Studies
   This document keeps track of leading information facilities in the field of Australian Aboriginal studies as well as the Indigenous
   Peoples studies.
Aeronautics and Aeronautical Engineering
African Studies
Agriculture
Animal health, wellbeing, and rights
Anthropology
Applied Linguistics
Archaeology
Architecture
Art
Asian Studies
Astronomy and Astrophysics

Document Done

FIGURE 16.1   World Wide Web Virtual Library Subject Guide

A Subject Guide for Chemistry

The Clearinghouse for Subject-Oriented Internet Resource Guides listing for chemistry, *Some Chemistry Resources on the Internet,* includes the following sources. You do not have to be a chemist to recognize that this list provides an invaluable resource for any chemistry-related search!

In the listing here, excerpted for simplicity, only one example is offered per heading. The full citations include relevant Internet addresses.

Book Catalogs
Chemistry Textbooks in Print Archive ...

Chemical Information Sources Guides
Chemistry Information. San Diego State University. "Chemistry Information" is an electronic reference source covering such topics as nomenclature, compound identification, properties, structure determination, toxicity, synthesis...

Databases
Periodic Table of the Elements (Physical Properties). University of California, Santa Barbara. An alphabetic listing of the elements with physical properties taken from the *CRC*

Handbook of Chemistry and Physics and Lange's *Handbook of Chemistry*...

Document Delivery
UnCover has tables of contents of many journals of interest to chemists. In addition, copies of articles can be ordered from the source...

E-mail Servers, Listservs, Newsgroups, etc.
CHEM-COMP, Computational Chemistry ...

FTP Resources
PACS, Physics and Astronomy Classification System. PACS is the thesaurus used in Physics Abstracts

Gophers
American Chemical Society Gopher. The ACS Gopher contains Supplementary Material pages from *Chemical Reviews,* the *Journal of the American Chemical Society* ...

Guides to Internet Resources
Chemistry Information on the Internet (Northern Illinois University)...

On-Line Search Services
DIALOG Online Chemistry Search Manua...

Periodicals and Conference Proceedings (Full Text)
Chemical Engineering Digest; ChE Electronic Newsletter...

Periodicals and Other Documents (Current Awareness)
Biochemistry Journals: Tables of Contents...

Software (Including Users Groups)
Macintosh Chemistry Tutorials...

Teaching Resources
Journal of Chemical Education Gopher...

World Wide Web Resources
World Wide Web Virtual Library: Crystallography...

KEY-WORD SEARCH PROGRAMS

When you have no idea where to start, one solution is to turn to key-word search programs. This solution, however, is not as simple as it might first appear.

Key-word search programs are particularly useful for finding unique names of persons or places (proper nouns) or specific terminology for which there is no synonym. The earlier carbonaceous chondrites (a form of meteorite) might be a candidate for a key-word search, although it is a bit specific. The term *meteors* might make more sense for an initial search. (Look up *chondrites* in a dictionary so that you can form a search term with some sagacity.)

Once you decide that a key-word search is appropriate, other decisions must be made. No single search program searches all of the Internet. Different search programs search different databases or search the same ones differently.

Some programs search titles or headers of documents, others search the documents themselves, still others search other indexes or directories. Some search the URLs (uniform resource locators) describing the location of a text, others the URLs embedded within hypertext pages. Finally, some search programs also search other databases, such as Gopher menus. Some search programs accept a single-word entry. Others allow you to use Boolean functions (AND, OR), limit the search to strings, and limit the number of items returned.

The outcome of seaches will vary in both the number of items found and the detail of the listings. The sheer number of citations may not be as meaningful as the accuracy and precision of the search. A large number of "hits" from mailing list correspondence may not be very productive.

A number of sites offer metasearch programs, a common format for a variety of search programs. A number of newer programs offer multisearch or parallel search capability, simultaneous searches by a number of search programs.

You must choose a particular search program and, with that, what to search and how. Again, your research must be guided by reflection.

The following is a listing of major key-word search programs.

Individual Programs—Index or List-Based

- YAHOO
  http://www.yahoo.com/search.html
  Extensive search options but cursory output. Nevertheless a powerful search tool for World Wide Web sites. (See Figure 16.2.)

- World Wide Web (CUI W3) Catalog: University of Geneva, Switzerland
  http://cuiwww.unige.ch/w3catalog

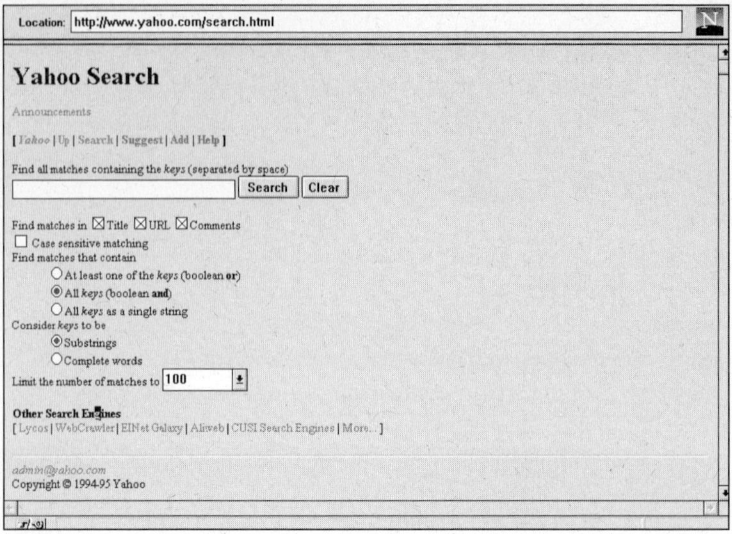

FIGURE 16.2   YAHOO World Wide Web Key-Word Search Program

Individual Programs—Automatically or Robot-Generated Databases

- Lycos (Carnegie Mellon University)
  http://lycos.cs.cmu.edu

  The largest automatically generated database. Includes World Wide Web, Gopher, and FTP files, as well as mailing lists. For many, the search program of choice. Returns extensively annotated listings with relevancy rankings in decreasing order.

- World Wide Web Worm
  http://www.cs.colorado.edu/home/mcbryan/WWWW.html
  Extensive search options; limited to Web sites, two-line output.

- WebCrawler (University of Washington)
  http://webcrawler.cs.washington.edu/WebQuery.html

Metasearch Programs
While these programs offer a unified format for inputting requests, they do not offer the options available at the program sites themselves.

- Internet Sleuth
  http://www.intbc.com/Sleuth
  Provides a common format for using a few search programs such as YAHOO and Lycos as well as links to close to five hundred searchable indexes and databases.

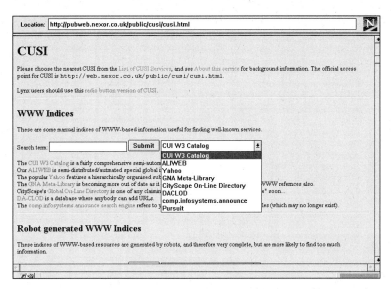

FIGURE 16.3 CUSI Common-Format Key-Word Search Program

- All-in-One Internet Search
  http://www.albany.net/~wcross/all1www.html#WWW
  Offers a common format for about twenty-five search programs.

- CUSI (Configurable Unified Search Interface) Twente University
  http://cui.www.unigue.ch or
  http://pubweb.nexor.co.uk/public/cusi/cusi.html
  Allows a choice of search program under various topic categories. (See Figure 16.3.)

- Amdahl Internet Exploration Page
  http://www.amdahl.com/internet/meta-index.html
  Includes many of the same programs as SavvySearch as well as access to multisearch programs.

- Quick Search
  http://gagme.wwa.com/~boba/search.html
  Simple searches of a wide variety of programs as well as access to multisearch programs.

Multisearch or Parallel Search Programs
While it might seem that these programs are the best options, remember that they compound the problems of all of the constituent programs and are only as fast as the slowest program selected. The options for the maximum time to wait for a response on the Multithread Query Gateway are from "five minutes" to "forever."

- SavvySearch, "the premier Parallel Internet Query Engine"
  http://www.cs.colostate.edu/~dreiling/smartform.html
  Offers simultaneous access to YAHOO, Lycos, Webcrawler, and other search programs generating a single result.
- Sun's Multithreaded Query Gateway
  http://www.sun.fi/mtq/mtquery.html
  This program is accessible through Amdahl and Quick Search above, as well as from *http://www.int.fuberlin.de./search/ mtquery.html.*

As might be expected, all of the major search programs are used extensively. After just a year on-line, YAHOO claimed twenty thousand users a day. It now receives half a million visits a day. Finally, do not forget Archie, Veronica, and WAIS, in both their native and World Wide Web manifestations.

FINDING SEARCH PROGRAMS

New search programs are being offered continually. Up-to-date listings of search programs and other research tools, with hypertext links for accessing each, can be obtained at the following sites:

The NCSA Internet Resources Meta-Index
http://www.ncsa.uiuc.edu/SDG/Software/Mosaic/MetaIndex.html

YAHOO Listing
http://www.yahoo.com/computers_and_internet/internet/world_wide_web

Searchable Resources Lists with Documentation
http://www.tamu.edu/global-info/search-plus-docs.html

 Excerpt from Lycos Search on "bagpipe"

Two of the search results are indicated here.

```
Found 85 documents containing at least one of these words:
bagpipe, bagpipe1, bagpiper, bagpipercxxfl, bagpipes
-----------------------------------------------------------
ID355211: [score 1.0000]
gopher://cs.dartmouth.edu/11/pub/bagpipes

date: 27-Nov-94
bytes: 1416
```

links: 11
keys: bagpipe bagpipes

excerpt:
Select one of:
* COCKNEY.WAV
* bagpipe-archive
* bagpipe-archive-92
* bagpipe-archive-93
* bagpipe-archive-94-1 * bagpipe-archive-94-2 * bagpipe-archive-94-3 * bagpipe.FAQ * cs * pipe-survey * very experimental Indexed Bagpipe archives

descriptions:
Bagpipe Archives - Dartmouth College Dept. of Computer Science
....
....
ID14696: [score 0.9218]
ftp://celtic.stanford.edu/pub/instruments/Bagpipe.FAQ

date: 10-Dec-94
bytes: 41272

keys: bagpipe bagpipes
excerpt:
Bagpipe.FAQ
Last modified on: 9/9/94 (MCS)
This file contains a number of Frequently Asked Questions (FAQ) from the bagpipe mailing list. Additionally, it contains information on topics of general interest to pipers, listeners, and other enthusiasts.
Some of the most common questions on the list are of the form "Does anyone have the address of pipe maker X or pipe supplier Z". Rather than embed addresses throughout the FAQ, an appendix of handy addresses and telephone numbers is provided at the end of this document.
CHANGES SINCE THE LAST REVISION (7/15/94):
Tidied up some typographical errors and corrected one or two faulty addresses. Clarified tips in section 3. Added several new addresses to the resource list. Thanks to the following people for their input

descriptions:
Bagpipe FAQ

TACTICS AND STRATEGIES

Assume you want to research slavery during the Civil War. As always, obvious starting points include encyclopedias and history books. But say you want to use the Internet. You might see what is available on a local desk reference menu or check the history resource listings at the Clearinghouse for Subject-Oriented Internet Resource Guides. If you do the latter via the World Wide Web, you can go directly to resources.

Alternatively, you could begin browsing through any of the other subject-area listings starting with humanities and proceeding through increasingly specific subject areas: history...American...Civil War...slavery...and so on.

Subject browsing provides a sense of the resources available. At each stage, further options for more specific investigation appear. If you used a key-word search for *slavery,* you might be deluged with entries relating to the Caribbean or ancient Egypt. If you restrict the search to *Civil War* and *slavery,* you would not discover unrelated material as you hone in on the topic. A search for information on a clearly unique topic, such as Abraham Lincoln, might be more fruitful with a key-word search, but you would still have to anticipate many citations and restrict your search to a particular aspect of his life.

The choice between Gopher and World Wide Web menus depends greatly on what you are looking for. If you need the graphic capability of the Web, so be it. Gopher menus on the other hand may run faster (especially on home computers) and be easier to traverse. These general inclinations should be tempered by the fact that a number of new and useful menus, especially related to business and leisure activities, appear solely on the Web. California State University has established the Web site CSU BIOWEB about everything biological (*http://arnica. csustan.edu*), and the chair of the computer-technology department at Indiana University-Purdue University at Indianapolis has a Web page pointing to thousands of commercial services (*http://www.engr.iupui.edu/~ho/interests/commmenu.html*).

When your interest can be easily defined by a specific search term, query the Veronica servers accessible through your local Gopher or use one of the search programs discussed earlier.

Feedback to Problems with Searches

If no results:

- Check spelling.
- Try more general terms.
- Try again with synonyms.
- Make sure the search program is not case sensitive.
- Use wild cards (such as *book** to include *books, booking, booked*)
- Try other search indexes.

If too many results:

- Try more specific terms.
- Restrict the search to combinations of terms (for example, x *.and.* y).
- Avoid common terms such as *university* and *html.*

In all cases, examine the specific rules for phrasing searches with each program.

IV

Issues

17

Controversy, Concerns, and Future Developments

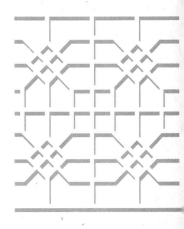

A ll modes of communication have social and political implications. The Internet is no exception.

THE FIRST AMENDMENT, PERSONAL RIGHTS, PUBLIC TASTE, AND CENSORSHIP

The Internet, it is often argued, is built on the First Amendment. One
does not have to own a publishing house or broadcast license to speak.
No central authority controls what anyone says. The Internet offers a
common forum for members of Congress, high school and college
students, the home-bound handicapped, seamstresses and sports fans,
scientists and gossips, politicians and soap opera fanatics.

In fact, the often-cited First Amendment view of the Internet is not
as pure as some might wish—or imagine. The mere presence of outrageous and scurrilous materials does not necessarily prove the absence
of censorship or deliberate selection. Universities have always exer-
cised control over files placed on their systems. In many discussion
groups, moderators decide what will or will not be posted—at times
more for political or personal reasons than criteria of suitability or
timeliness. Internet providers select the discussion groups available
on their system. Access to file transfer protocols is often limited geo-
graphically, and certain users have priority during busy periods
(anonymous users come last).

Regrettably, not all people are well informed, responsible, or even sensitive to others' feelings. Small, isolated, cash-strapped hate groups have found the Internet an enticing vehicle for distributing their message. Officials of the Simon Wiesenthal Center in Los Angeles, leaders in antidiscrimination causes, have expressed concern for the extent of bigoted and hate-oriented materials on the Internet. But who will censor? What is to be censored? For what purpose and at what cost? Here as elsewhere, there is a thin line between maintaining standards of civility and censorship, between freedom of expression and responsible discussion.

Historically, policing of the Internet has been done by the users themselves. Participants have attempted to maintain an etiquette ("netiquette") respecting each others' interests and feelings. Users have punished those who post advertisements on newsgroups by deluging their mailbox with messages (spamming). Groups of user-vigilantes have systematically erased messages posted to an inordinate number of newsgroups.

As family-oriented on-line services increasingly offer access to the resources of the Internet, the content of those resources has come under greater scrutiny. Legally, the Internet operates in a gray area between public speech and personal communication. Courts have held that the Internet qualifies as a "common carrier" much like the telephone company. Those offering access cannot be held liable for what passes over their lines. How long this will last is not clear. In June 1995, a New York State judge ruled that the on-line service Prodigy qualified as a publisher, responsible for libelous messages posted on its service, on the grounds that it tried to maintain editorial control by scanning for obscenities. At the same time, various parent

> In 1974, the American Historical Association issued a Statement of Professional Standards endorsing "candor, forcefulness, or persistence" in the expression of differences of opinion. It rejected "civility" on the grounds that it would interfere with free debate.
> Jesse Lemisch, "Point of View," *Chronicle of Higher Education*, January 20, 1995.

groups put forth proposals for rating systems incorporated into Internet files and software to enable parents to control children's access to specific material.

National politicians, of course, jumped on the bandwagon of correctness and family values. On March 23, 1995, the U.S. Senate Commerce Committee approved a bill (*S. 314*) that held companies distributing "obscene, lewd, lascivious, or filthy" material on computer systems subject to fines up to $100,000 or jail terms up to two years. The legislation applied both to files distributed on global services and to E-mail messages. Speaker of the House Newt Gingrich, himself the author of a somewhat racy novel, supported a more sophisticated balance between the free speech of adults and the protection of children. In August, the House passed a telecommunications bill merely encouraging managers of networks to purge system of indecent material. And by a margin of 420 to 4, the House approved an amendment that prohibited the Federal Communications Commission from regulating the content of material on the Internet and absolved network managers from liability for material on their systems. With a presidential election year coming, however, the issue seemed far from dead.

ANONYMITY, LICENSE, AND SECURITY

Another area of debate involves the question of anonymity. Anonymity can evoke candor on touchy topics. It can provide an opportunity for an unbiased hearing to some who might not gain one otherwise. It also may be appropriate for subscribers to some mailing lists, such as to AIDS newsletters.

> "Almighty God, Lord of all life, we praise you for the advancements in computerized communication that we enjoy in our time.... Now, guide the Senators as they consider ways of controlling the pollution of computer communications and how to preserve one of our greatest resources: the minds of our children and the future moral strength of our Nation. Amen."
>
> Senate prayer by the Chaplain, Dr. Lloyd John Ogilvie, June 12, 1995.

But anonymity can also be used irresponsibly to hide one's true identity or to sully someone else's reputation. While various aspects of the Internet ask for a username or Internet address as identification, true identities can be easily forged. (It is harder with on-line services that require a means of billing.) Various "anonymous re-mailers" will forward mail, and hence postings to newsgroups and mailing lists, anonymously, stripping all identification. This practice has not gone unchallenged. On February 8, 1995, Finnish police successfully served a summons demanding the address of an anonymous user from the director of one of the most famous sites, *anon.penet.fi.*

The flipside of anonymity might be impersonation. Enterprising computer wizards have found ways to disguise their Internet addresses (and with that their Internet identities) to fool computers into providing them access. A classic *New Yorker* cartoon portrays a dog sitting at a computer successfully posing as a human on the Internet.

A related issue involves assuring the security of transmissions. Internet transmissions follow circuitous paths from one computer to another. Any computer along the way can intercept messages. Internet administrators can capture the address of callers for later promotional campaigns—the Internet equivalent of junk mailing lists. Network administrators can maintain a "click-stream," or transaction log, of a user's on-line activities, with the subsequent potential for harassment, humiliation, or outright blackmail.

Concerned about communication by terrorists, the federal government has sought to assure its ability to wiretap new modes of communication technology. Developing such a capability has proved a problem. Not only has there been vocal outrage at potential governmental abuse, but the coding device proposed was soon cracked. Nevertheless, the terrorist bombing of the Federal Building in Oklahoma City in April of 1995 provided additional impetus and support for future governmental access to electronic communication technology.

Issues of anonymity and impersonation take on greater importance with the increasing commercial use of the Internet. For commerce to be successful (see box below), users must be able to authenticate identities and assure the privacy of personal and financial information. Encryption would seem to solve the problem, but for messages to be encrypted, the coding must be agreed upon by both sender and recipient and must be secure. Various proposals for secure transmission and verification have been proposed–tamperproof electronic envelopes sealed with digital fingerprints, as it were. But while some support the Digital Signature Standard (DSS), other groups endorse Digital ID.

Finally, it is not clear how the protection of copyright can be maintained when documents are published on the Internet, just as it is not clear how one can prevent tampering with a manuscript on the Internet. When you pick up a book or newspaper, you have a certain confidence in the authenticity of the material. On the Internet, you may not be so sure. Numerous efforts to encode a digital watermark within data to identify and guarantee authorship are therefore being proposed. (We might note in passing that while commercial data services make money providing access to documents in journals and other sources, the authors of those documents do not benefit financially.)

PRIVATIZATION AND COMMERCIALIZATION

The Internet was developed initially under government sponsorship as a vehicle for academics and researchers. An "acceptable use policy" banned commercial use. In later years, the National Science Foundation eased the restrictions on transmissions on its lines to allow new product announcements but not advertising–and then only in support or research and education. Privatization and commercialization of the Internet now looms as the greatest test of the system's evolutionary stability.

In many ways, the future of on-line services is apparent in the new players. Sears Roebuck and IBM own Prodigy; H&R Block owns CompuServe; General Electric owns Genie; AT&T owns the Interchange Network Company and Imagination Network game system. AT&T, Microsoft, IBM, and Sony are all expected to offer their own full-service access to the Internet. Previously independent Internet software producers and administrators of nonprofit programs have increasingly signed large commercial contracts. Both the YAHOO and EINet Galaxy World Wide Web search programs have contracted to accept advertising, and major on-line companies continue to purchase the wares of Internet suppliers. CompuServe Information Services has purchased Spry Inc., the largest supplier of Internet software. Microsoft has contracted with UUNET Technologies to establish a World Wide Web dial-up network and obtained a license to use NCSA Mosaic software. American Online has purchased rights to the Global Network Navigator search program.

In addition, the physical network of the Internet is increasingly in private hands. On May 13, 1995, the National Science Foundation's NSFnet was phased out in favor of a commercially owned backbone connecting major computing centers. Previously nonprofit regional networks serving business, government, and academic institutions have been purchased by commercial networks. National telephone companies are positioning themselves as Internet network providers. As the physical network is placed in commercial hands, many predict that per-packet transmission fees will soon follow.

Other traditional limits on the commercialization of the Internet have also begun to give way. With the demise of NSF's acceptable use policy, the Internet was used to announce new products. Order taking soon followed. The year 1995 saw initial experiments with digital cash such as DigiCash and Cyber-Cash, encrypted credit card numbers, and various transaction security programs, all in anticipation of on-line shopping networks not unlike those on cable television.

In some ways, there is no reason for concern here. The rapid expansion of the Internet requires an infusion of additional capital if the Internet is to meet growing needs. But the needs and offerings are changing and, in the eyes of some, seriously compromised. For many, the Internet struggles to maintain an identity of high intellectual purpose, to keep the forces of home-buyer-network television and the

---

Find a Friend

REUNITE with long lost relatives or friends

GET BACK IN TOUCH with research colleagues

FIND college or high school alumni

SEARCH OUT your veteran friends

MAKE CONTACT with your biological Mom or Dad

COLLECT on an old debt

The above is from the home page for Find a Friend (*http:/www.ais.net:80/findafriend*). The company tracks people using public and proprietary sources including credit card companies, phone directories, court records, and magazine circulation departments. The charge is $18 a search, no charge if they fail. An innovative use of resources or an Orwellian attack on privacy? It's your call.

---

video game arcade at bay. For others, this is simply the evolution of the Internet as a medium of multimedia entertainment and commerce. Only time will tell whether the new commercialism represents a new opportunity or the degradation of an existing medium.

OTHER INHERENT PROBLEMS AND CONCERNS

The Internet also faces technological issues. The greatest concern here might be the problem of saturation. While a single word may take only fifty bits of information and a single picture five thousand to five hundred thousand bits, one second of video requires fifty million bits. Attempts to increase the bandwidth—the volume and speed of transmissions—are constantly underway in an effort to deal with the skyrocketing number of new users and the serious deterioration of the speed of the system due to the heavy load imposed by multimedia applications. For some, the only way to regain control is to charge for usage, whether on the basis of the amount of material or the priority of the transmission.

The major issues of the future, however, may be of a more social nature, involving questions of equity and usefulness. In principle, everyone has equal access to the resources of the Internet. Just as there is a gap between the educated and the illiterate, a gap remains between those who have access and those who do not, between those for whom the information is available and those unable to afford the necessary equipment and linkage. While many argue that privatization will foster competition that will lower prices, it is not clear how marginal access will be maintained.

The much vaunted sense of community on the Internet has been challenged. Rather than offering true personal communication in real-life situations with a broad segment of the population, the Internet still involves interactions with a like-minded social stratum comprised mostly of

LITZLER

"ALL THIS E-MAIL... I MISS SCHMOOZING."

upper-middle-class white males. On an international level, countries with non-Latin alphabets struggle to become involved.

Finally, there is the question of the content and, with that, the value of the product itself. The number of new items added each week is staggering. One can spend hours surfing, searching, lurking, leering, and, one hopes, discovering. Yet much of the current material is outdated, dispersed, or only offers snippets of information. Much of the discussion on newsgroups is simply chatter or static more appropriate to "Geraldo"-type television shows.

Some have forecast that digital technology will be a natural force drawing people into greater world harmony.* Others foresee the ultimate demise of the Internet as a "mishmash of technologies that is going to dribble out over the years."† Alternatively, a schism may ultimately develop between a new academic/research Internet and a corporate-sponsored multimedia entertainment cyberspace controlled by cable television companies.

*Nicholas Negroponte, *Being Digital*, Knopf, 1995.

†Danny Goodman, *Living at Light Speed: Your Survival Guide to the Information Highway*, Random House, 1995.

> "If the Internet is no longer free, people would be forced to decide how much they really value it. In many cases, the answer seems to be 'not much.'"
>
> Charles C. Mann, "Is the Internet Doomed?" *Inc. Technology*, 1995, No. 2.

> "It's an unreal universe, a soluble tissue of nothingness. While the Internet beckons brightly, seductively flashing an icon of knowledge-as-power, this non-place lures us to surrender our time on earth."
>
> Clifford Stoll, *Silicon Snake Oil: Second Thoughts on the Information Highway*, Doubleday, 1995.

Appendices

Some Computer Basics

Text Versus Graphic Displays

Commands Versus Point and Click

Unix

Shareware and Commercial Software

Files

Viruses

Directories and Subdirectories

Computing Versus Housekeeping

Choices and Limits

File Storage Formats

Encoding Files

Archiving Files

Compressing Files

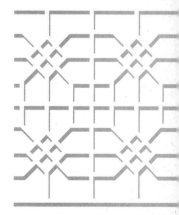

Text Versus Graphic Displays

On early computers, lines of type snaked across a black and white screen. The most exciting computer game involved keeping a cursor bouncing like a ping pong ball on an otherwise blank screen. Today, computer screens resemble the latest in amusement arcades. They display thousands of shades of color and movie-like animation.

The increasing complexity of computer images is made possible in part by faster computer chips and advances in monitor technology. The appearance of the screen depends, however, primarily on the operating system, the basic programming of the computer, not the monitor. The resulting appearance is referred to as the interface, since it is the means by which the user interfaces with the computer.

Text interface, or more accurately, command line interface, mimics the output of a typewriter. You can create documents that will print different sizes and styles of type, but you cannot display those fonts on the screen. While the screen may be in color, it is limited to twenty-four or forty-eight lines eighty characters wide and the characters on the keyboard. Text interface is commonly associated with MS-DOS (Microsoft's Disk Operating System).

Newer operating systems offer a *graphic interface* (or GUI–graphical user interface). Icons and other symbols are apparent. (For a vivid example of the difference between interfaces, compare the transcript of FTP access in Chapter 8 with the graphic-interface screen in Figure 8.1.) Word processor text appears on screen as it would if printed– "what you see is what you get" (abridged to the delightful acronym WYSIWYG, pronounced *wiss-ee-wig*). Graphic displays are associated with Microsoft Windows (actually an add-on to DOS), IBM OS/2, and Apple Macintosh operating systems.

Commands Versus Point and Click

The difference between graphic and text interface is not limited to how the screen looks. It affects the use of the computer itself. The only way to move around the screen with a text interface is to follow the lines on the page with cursor keys–left and right, up and down. Graphic interface frees the cursor to roam at will and gives rise to the mouse (not the rodent!–but the device you slide around on the desk to move the cursor) and tracball (essentially an upside-down mouse). Text interface is based on commands and cursor keys. Graphic interface uses a "point and click" approach: highlight an icon or other image and click a button on the mouse or tracball.

While the trend is obviously toward graphic systems, each has advantages. It is easier to click on icons than to remember the specific commands and syntax required by a text-based system. On the same computer, however, a text-based system will generally display information faster than a graphic system since the text screen requires less information. Ultimately, of course, while text and graphic interfaces differ in looks and operation, programs in the different systems do pretty much the same thing. All mail programs, for instance, offer essentially the same options and services. All of the services on the Internet can be accessed with either text-based or graphics software.

Unix

MS-DOS, Windows, OS/2, and Macintosh System 7 are not the only operating systems–they are merely the ones most often associated with personal computers. Other operating systems include X-Windows, NeXT, VMS, and Unix. Unix was used in the early development of the Internet and remains the protocol required for issuing commands on command line Internet systems. Like MS-DOS, Unix confronts the user with a prompt, usually *%*.

Shareware and Commercial Software

The term *hardware* refers to physical objects such as computers, printers, and monitors. *Software* refers generally to the programs run on a computer.

Software exists in physical form on floppy disks and hard drives, but its essence is in the creative process. Software is intellectual property, like a story or a song. It is subject to copyright laws and with that to restrictions on its use.

Software is distributed in various ways with varying restrictions. Commercial software is marketed as a money-making endeavor. It is illegal to copy or transmit it without explicit permission. Public domain software, on the other hand, is not subject to copyright. There are no restrictions on its use and distribution. Public domain software is available free on bulletin boards, on-line services, and the Internet. Freeware is similar to public domain software insofar as it is available without restriction to all users, but the original author maintains the copyright and hence intellectual (as opposed to physical) ownership. Software developed under the auspices of federal or other grants might be distributed as freeware.

Shareware refers to programs available free–but only on a trial basis. Users are expected to send a payment if they continue use beyond an initial trial period. With formal registration, users often receive the latest version, documentation, technical support, and the removal of on-screen registration reminders. While often mistaken for freeware, shareware is really commercial software that is distributed in an innovative way. Demos are abbreviated forms of commercial software programs, usually limited in the number or size of file they can handle–or in some function, such as the ability to print or save files. All of the above forms of software except commercial versions are available on national on-line services as well as the Internet.

While shareware and freeware are available without charge, they are not necessarily inferior to commercial software. Both the initial World Wide Web browser, Mosaic, and a major successor, Netscape, are available as shareware. The premier mail program, Eudora, is available both as shareware (version 1.4.4) and as a commercial product (version 2.0).

Finally, the term vaporware is applied to software that has been announced by a producer before it exists or that is far behind schedule. The term is more derisive than descriptive. Vaporware is always faster, more versatile, and more error-free than existing programs. While vaporware may simply represent the unrealistic hopes of a manufacturer, it may also be an attempt to limit sales of competitive software.

The last few years have seen a growing tendency of companies involved in the development of client/server software to make the client portion available free. The Web browser Netscape, the audio player RealAudio, and the document reader Adobe Acrobat are all being marketed in this way.

Files

Computer information is stored in electronic form as files on floppy disks or internal hard drives. Files may contain programs, text, numerical data, graphic images, or sound files. To a computer's memory, all files are the same. The nature of the file is usually indicated by the extension, a three-letter code following a period in the name.

Common Sound and Graphic File Extensions

Sound Files

.SBI	Sound Blaster Instrument
.SND	Macintosh Sounder/Soundtools
.WAV	Microsoft Windows Waveform
.VOC	SoundBlaster
.AV	Unix-Based NeXT/Sun

Still Image Files

.BMP	Bitmap
.GIF	Graphics Interchange Format
.JPEG	Joint Photographic Experts Group
.PCD	Kodak Photo CD
.PNG	Portable Network Graphics (soon to replace GIF)
.PS	postscript
.TIFF	Tagged Image File Format
.WPG	WordPerfect Graphic

Motion Picture/Animation Files

.AVI	Audio Video Interleaved
.FLI	Flick
.GL	Grasp animation
.MOV	Macintosh QuickTime
.MPG	MPEG (similar to JPEG)

Viruses

The same ingenuity used to create complex software programs
has been used to create computer viruses, programs that attach themselves to other programs. When executed, the infected programs de-
stroy files and/or disrupt normal computer operation. The damage
may be minimal (a message on your screen) or devastating (the dele-
tion of all files on your hard drive). Any executable files introduced
into your computer via a floppy disk or modem may carry a virus.

   Viruses may appear infrequently, but they do appear. Caution is
warranted. On-line services and bulletin boards screen their files for
viruses, but they cannot always catch the most recent versions. As a
broader and more decentralized network, the Internet may not be as
safe.

   Programs to detect and erase viruses are available commercially
or as shareware or freeware on the Internet. Scan all files periodically
or individual files as they are written to your computer–and always
back up your files … just in case.

Directories and Subdirectories

Files are stored in directories and subdirectories, much like papers
within file folders within drawers within file cabinets. Directory structure is often displayed as a subdirectory "tree":

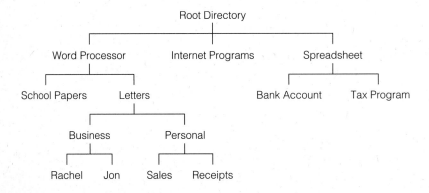

To locate a particular file, move through the subdirectory structure
with commands that change to a specific directory or return you to the
root directory.

Computing Versus Housekeeping

Using a computer, we create, store, and retrieve files. We open files to read them and save them with any changes when we're done. We may copy a file to a floppy disk or print its contents to paper. The major computer commands, after all, are not add and subtract, compute the mean and estimate the standard deviation. They are more often housekeeping commands such as *copy* and *delete, create a directory,* and *list the files in a directory.*

The activities described above are more a matter of browsing than creating, more a matter of fussing with folders than fussing with ideas—all of which is to prepare you for the realization that negotiating the Internet is mostly a matter of negotiating directory trees and menus. It does not require a rocket scientist. The activities are quite straightforward. What you choose to do with what you find is the tough part.

Choices and Limits

You are working away on a computer. Text or graphic material appears on the screen. What do you do?

As suggested, most of the work on a computer does not involve acts of great creativity. When you write a letter, construct a spreadsheet, or draw a picture, you must be imaginative. In most other situations, you simply respond to a set of predetermined options, whether specific menu options or the choice of available commands. Prompts (e.g., C:\>) may seem open-ended, but there are just so many legitimate commands that you can enter. Some systems, for instance, accept *delete,* others demand *erase*–and you cannot erase a file that does not exist.

File Storage Formats

As noted earlier, files can be stored in various formats. The following sentence is composed solely of keyboard characters:

This is an ordinary sentence, with no fancy elements.

Such a sentence would be stored in ASCII (American Standard Code for Information Interchange) format, the "plain vanilla" or unformatted text format. It is composed essentially of the keyboard characters: upper- and lowercase letters, numbers, punctuation marks, and some additional signs. All type size and font indications are absent.

The following text was composed with a word processor:

This is a sentence with **boldface**, *italics*, and underlining.

Various display attributes are present here–different type sizes and boldface and italic fonts. To capture this added information, such files are stored in binary format, a format readable only by computers:

```
WPCiⁿ  ⁿ
ⁿ      ⁿ ▶            ⁿⁿ  ▶    ≡  #ⁿ   *ⁿ   ⁿ            ℅ⁿ   ↑   *ⁿ   Uⁿ   ×
§ⁿ  δⁿⁿ   (   ?ⁿ  U♥   F   gⁿ

◙3¦  `   ⁿ  Cⁿ     ⁿEpson  LX-810  ½ⁿ      ┬ⁿ#      Xⁿⁿ ,ⁿⁿ Xⁿ       x è
ⁿ•   ┬ⁿ  t EPLX810.PRS  *       XⁿXⁿ       ↑
                           Hᴸ      ⁿ↔{tδ└uDⁿ ♦ Xⁿ2 ∈←\‡→          ◄       ⁿ
    `  +ⁿ ▶‡ Roman        ⁿ  ♦ (                 ⁿ‡ⁿ $ í   í   +←♀‡
◄        ⁿ pÉ ←ⁿ å¶. Dutch  801  Bold  Speedo         ▌
▶ âⁿ  ♥    !▶ ∥δ
  ♥
 ▌ThisÇisÇaÇ └ↄ  çⁿ♦ Xⁿ4-♦ Xⁿ  Xⁿ" Xⁿᵃ½ⱴ  └└ↄⱴ  çⁿ♦ äⱴ4-♦ äⱴ∞ⁿXⁿ◄ Xⁿ4-ⱴ  └sente
nce └ↄ# âⁿ♦ Xⁿ4-♦ Xⁿgⁿäⱴ◄ äⱴ4-Nⱴ  #  └└ↄ# âⁿ♦ Xⁿᵃ½  Xⁿ∞ⁿXⁿ◄ Xⁿ4-╱ⱴ  #  └ÇwithÇ
≥♀≥boldface≤♀≤,Ç≥italics≤ÇandÇ≥ⱊ≥underlining≤ⱊ≤.
```

Technically, "binary" means utilizing zeros and ones, but here it implies a particular set of characters that goes beyond those included in the ASCII set. This format includes additional characters such as Ÿ and Ç. (The ASCII set is composed of 128 7-bit characters, the binary set of 256 8-bit characters.) All executable or program files are stored in binary format.

Encoding Files

Files can be transferred between computers in various ways. One of the most common means of transfer is via electronic mail (E-mail). But E-mail files must be in ASCII format; binary files cannot be sent via E-mail. How then can word processor text be transmitted?

Binary text files can of course be reformatted as plain ASCII text, but the display attributes would be lost. The solution to the transmission problem involves encoding the files utilizing ASCII characters. The earlier word processor file encoded with the program Wincode appears as follows:

```
section 1/1   file abc.wp   [ Wincode v2.6.1 ]

begin 644 abc.wp
M_U=00ZT"```!"@(``````(`$`````````````"`(!```$``````/`````(
M(P$P$$`^``````````````````````````````````````````````````(
M(`(#0D8````!ER``````````````````````````````````````````````
```

Notice that the characters are now all ASCII characters. The information necessary for the fonts and display attributes can be recaptured by decoding the file back into binary format.

Files can be encoded and decoded using various protocols. Each such protocol is indicated by a file extension. Uuencode (illustrated above) results in *.uue files.

Archiving Files

A number of files can be joined, packed, or "archived" into a single file. The most common programs for combining files are the Unix program *tar* (**.tar*) and MS-DOS/Windows PKZIP/PKUNZIP and Macintosh ZipIt (**.ZIP*) programs. Archived files must be unpacked before use. Archiving enables you to transfer a number of files, or all files in a directory, with a single command.

Compressing Files

Files can also be compressed to shorten transmission time or to simply save on storage space. The earlier word processor file is compressed here using the standard PKZIP (**.ZIP*) protocol, which combines archiving and compression. Notice again that this is a binary file.

```
PK♥♦¶    ¶ja▲(1J▲=⊡  ù♥  ♦    ABC.WP=R▀N⁴p¶■~▌ ᴸn,▐-ÄÉU♥8M♀▌▌)‡n3◄θ^▶│Çã^×AYð▫d■
Γ▐∥θé‡M§Éxσ+×▐=bΓ#†Ŕan{θì1⌐♥ ᴸnæ‡Ç»=_0ᴸ■▪∥i▬Λ·«θ*K"4Σq♦]Sd▐"ò∏∥⁴M      QZÄDↆ‡
ïñᴶ§ZáLSÜċën1σyΓKæ^R┌►n†·│0†ûcbE=ëÄia*=ᵒT├ᴸnaóé♠ℛċ┬5hHθᴸfᵣrⓇkr→KJ±)n8>ᴸ‡ᴸ€α•pªΓ
†▐∥Zs▌ 1ᴸkᵣᵞ▐&ªpæb^ᴸy♠1n#^²¶U≈♣²  ≈·½
ì˜≤Sⁿ1 ▐§KↆáÉß"∏▐H‡▌ᴸ1}Ç┤Q]B∏£N■}↔¬ċß†ᴶQ‼YänΣèð·y┤┛»θ¶ÄnU▐è>ì┤▬ᴮß=←ᴸz¥▐/┼Ñð¢ᵣ&Wᴨ
=▐∥ì◄ì∥yìfΚ·¥ᵖ≤†ì&▐ôg1z⁴q{θo+†ûfqó├í≤ᴸᾱ⧉t▐,S{θ9↔∥b84.▐Gᵣσ▬†·η2‡B‡Lⱳ±¦∥k9Cúîᴨ ⌐┤
┤ûT!Iz=ûeU*IH:    9↔Hô½J0┤Cé}∥n♦a.▪ᴵ∅ᵣn1û‼σóÑ ᴸC╟∥n¼‡θQ`yⱴ▶Nã}ᴸ⌴ⱴ⟩ⱴ]ᴸ⌍ᵣᴛdT² •PKθ
θ¶ ¶    ¶ja▲(1J▲=⊡  ù♥  ♦              ABC.WPPK♦♠      ⊡ ⊡ 4  ±⊡
```

The compression ratio varies with the type of file. Program files generally compress to about half the size (2:1), data files more than 5:1. In this case, the word processor file was 919 bytes; the compressed file is now 571 bytes. (By contrast, the initial ASCII version was 60 bytes.)

The Unix compress/uncompress program (**.Z*) is often used in conjunction with the archiver *tar*, resulting in files of the form **.tar.Z*.

Common Archive/Compression Formats

SUFFIX	PROGRAM
.Hqx	HQX (Macintosh)
.lzh	LHa, LHarc, Larc
.shar	SHell ARchive (mostly Unix)
.sit	Stuff-It (Macintosh)
.tar	Tape ARchive (mostly Unix)
.uue	uuencode/uudecode (also .uu)
.Z	compress (mostly Unix, seen in combination with tar as .tar.Z files)
.zip	Zip (either PKZip or Zip/Unzip)

A complete list of file compression/archiving methods and the programs to uncompress/unarchive is available from *ftp://ftp.cso.uiuc.edu/doc/pcnet/compression.* See also "How To Undecode and View Binary Messages" on the Usenet newsgroups *alt.binaries.pictures.d* and *new.newusers.questions..*

Getting on
the Internet

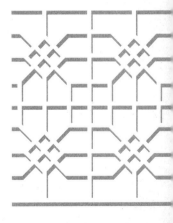

You've read enough. You want to get on the 'Net. What should you do next? First of all, talk to friends and associates. Find out what they are "on." This is a marvelous way to evaluate on-line services or Internet providers. What troubles have they had? How much do they actually use it? What are they really getting out of it? What is it costing per month? Their experience may not truly reflect yours, but it may be a good guide.

Peruse recent computer magazines. *Internet World* and *The Net* offer wide-ranging discussion of current issues and developments. *Wired* addresses a broad audience interested in all aspects of multimedia communication. *Online Access* and *NetGuide* emphasize new sites on the Internet and on-line services. Consider any magazine with *PC, Windows,* or *Macintosh* in the title. All of these magazines regularly provide information on new programs and sites, as well as advertisements by national Internet providers.

However you decide to go on-line, the initial requirement is a computer with modem. Just about any computer will do, although newer, faster computers are highly advantageous. A 14,400-baud modem is a necessity for graphic-interface programs; a 2,400-baud modem will work for text interface, but downloading will be excruciatingly slow.

THE OPTIONS

You can get an initial flavor of the Internet by dialing in to local or national bulletin boards. They are for the most part free and offer an introduction to many of the same types of services. Check your local library or computer store for phone numbers.

Internet access itself is available in a variety of ways. Essentially, you need a network connection through an Internet service provider—a "gateway" providing an "on ramp" to the Internet, in modern parlance—which you can obtain via a business or institutional network hookup or by telephone to a local or national provider. More specifically, the options are as follows:

- on-line services
- shell accounts
- SLIP/PPP (Serial Line Internet Protocol and Point-to-Point-Protocol) accounts
- direct network access

If you are accessing the Internet at a major corporation, government facility, or academic institution, direct network access may be available. If that is the case, jump to the final option. If not, read on.

Nonnetwork access requires a telephone link to a provider. National on-line companies and Internet providers offer local numbers for most cities and regions. Rural areas are obviously less extensively served. Some providers may offer an 800 number, but there might be an additional charge. Finally, many cities have local Internet providers. In most cases, free trial accounts are available.

On-line Services

This first option for accessing the Internet is the easiest for the beginner at home. America Online, CompuServe, Prodigy, and eWorld all offer access to all Internet services (see Figure B.1). Each provides all the proprietary software necessary to use the service. What you gain is simplicity of operation. You pay with limits on the resources available and the expense of sizeable on-line charges if you exceed the monthly allotment.

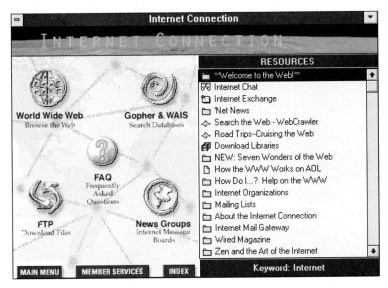

FIGURE B.1   America Online Internet Menu

Shell Accounts

Shell accounts are offered by hundreds of local and national providers as well as by local bulletin boards. You are not really on the Internet yourself, merely connected to someone who is. You use the software programs of the provider. This basic service is cheap (roughly $10 to $20 per month) but usually limited to text-interface applications, making this the most difficult option to use. Files are downloaded first to the provider computer and then to your own machine, an awkward two-step procedure.

SLIP/PPP

The third approach is through a more direct line to the Internet via a SLIP (Serial Line Internet Protocol) or PPP (Point-to-Point Protocol) account from a local or national provider. (SLIP is simply a TCP/IP protocol designed for telephone lines.) Files are downloaded directly to your own computer rather than to an intermediary.

SLIP/PPP access is offered by local and national Internet service providers. You will need TCP/IP interface software, such as Trumpet WINSOCK or MacTCP, plus individual programs such as Mosaic or Netscape for the World Wide Web, HGopher for Gopher programs, Eudora for E-mail, and so on. Software can be acquired in various ways:

- *Individual freeware or shareware programs* are available on the Internet. While such programs can be state of the art, set-up can be tricky, and the documentation is often limited. Integrated "suites" of shareware programs with a common interface are also available, but the individual applications are usually weaker than self-standing programs. Shareware programs such as The Internet Starter Kit for Windows are often packaged with relatively expensive Internet manuals.

- *Suites of commercial software* are available for around $100. These include Spry's Internet in a Box, MKS's Internet Anywhere, NetManager's Internet Chameleon, Software Venture's Internet Valet for Macintosh, Wollongong's Emissary, Quarterdeck's Internet Suite, and InterAp's California Software. Commercial suites generally provide simple steps for enrolling with national Internet service providers. Enter your credit card number and the program configures your connection, but often at a monthly access fee significantly higher than available locally. Programs such as Netscape Navigator Personal Edition augment a World Wide Web browser with additional programs for sending E-mail and reading newsgroups, with the same convenient means of accessing major Internet service providers.

- *Software integrated into the operating system* is offered by IBM's OS/2 Warp and Microsoft's Windows 95.
- *National Internet providers* such as NetCom, PSINet, I-Link, and Pipelines, and even some national on-line services, provide proprietary suites of software limited to their systems.
- As a last resort, the graphic interface of a SLIP account can be mimicked on a local shell account with software such as Slip-Knot and The Internet Adapter.

Network Access

The final–and, when available, the best–option is direct access via a network or other leased line. If you are with a university, business, government, or private organization that has a direct, full-time hookup, you have only to link into that network. Network connection is equivalent to having a SLIP account. You must still have client software on your computer. This is the only real option for a nonintermittent link, and speeds of 10 megabytes per second are often available, since your modem is replaced by the network hardware.

Caveat Emptor: Not All Providers Are Equal

Before committing to a specific Internet service provider, remember:

Not all providers offer all Internet services.

Most providers offer free trial periods or guest accounts.

Many providers can supply the necessary software.

Monthly and on-line fees will vary; calculate potential fees for your anticipated usage.

Help with setup and continuing support will vary.

Not all providers can support fast modems.

Too few phone lines can result in busy signals.

Long-term contracts are cheaper only if you have a long-term commitment.

Some providers allow you to post a World Wide Web home page free of charge.

RECOMMENDATIONS

If insecure about your computer abilities or uneasy about your commitment to the Internet, sign up for a trial enrollment with America Online. When your monthly bill exceeds the minimum payment, shift to Netscape Navigator Personal Edition and where possible enroll with a local Internet provider. For serious use, assemble your own suite from shareware on the Internet.

InterNIC Internet Service Providers List [United States]

An up-to-date list of U.S.-based Internet access providers is available via E-mail from *ftpmail@decwrl.dec.com*. Use no subject and send this message:

connect ftp.colossus.net

dir

get list

quit

For out-of-the-way access, have a friend post a message on the newsgroup *alt.internet.access-wanted*.

Glossary

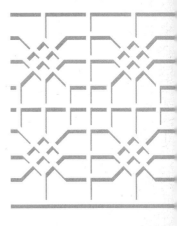

Advanced Research Projects Agency Network (ARPAnet)
An experimental computer network, developed by the U.S. Defense Department Advanced Research Projects Agency in the 1960s, utilizing packet switching and translation to a common transmission language. The precursor to the Internet.

America Online   One of the top three national on-line services.

Analog (adjective)   Involving a continuous and infinite set of values, as opposed to digital. The volume and tone controls on a radio are analog in nature; the channel selection on a television is digital. Computers are digital devices. See also **Digital.**

Anonymous FTP   A file retrieval program with a common public password. See also **File Transfer Protocol.**

Archie   A search program providing listings of the locations of files available by anonymous FTP. Also the automated indexing program upon which such searches are based.

Archive (verb)   To combine two or more files into one.

Archive site   A computer that stores and provides access to a specific collection of files.

ARPAnet   See **Advanced Research Projects Agency Network.**

ASCII file   A file encoding format, developed by the American Standard Code for Information Interchange, that represents upper- and lowercase letters, numbers, punctuation marks, and basic operations (for example, tab, enter) by numbers from 1 to 128. A file encoded in standard keyboard characters—as opposed to a binary file. An unformatted text file. See also **Binary file**.

Backbone   The top level in a computer network, characterized by a high transfer rate.

Binary   Represented by ones and zeros, for example, 11001001.

Binary file   A file encoded in binary code. More often, a file encoded with characters including but not limited to those found on a standard keyboard. Executable programs are stored as binary or nontext files.

Bit (binary digit)   A single unit of data.

bps   Bits per second.

Browser   Specifically, a program for reading the Hypertext Markup Language of World Wide Web pages. More generally, any program for following a path of menu items or other links.

Bulletin board system (BBS)
An on-line computer network offering information and mes-

sages. Generally nonprofit and local or interest-group focused. See also **On-line service**.

Byte   Eight bits. The number of bits necessary to indicate a single number or letter of the alphabet.

CD-ROM (Compact Disk–Read Only Memory)   A computer memory device utilizing the same technology as music compact disks (CDs).

Cello   A popular World Wide Web browser developed at Cornell University.

Chat   A program or forum for on-line group discussion.

Client   A computer system, program, or user that requests services from another computer, the server, on a network. See also **Server.**

Command Line Interface   A form of text interface in which new data is displayed line by line instead of page by page. See also **Text interface.**

Compression   The reduction in the size of a file to achieve a smaller storage space or faster transmission.

CompuServe (CompuServe Information Services–CIS) One of the top three national on-line services, noted especially for business information and services.

CRIS   A bulletin board of bulletin boards providing access to national bulletin boards via a local telephone call.

Cyberspace   The electronic "world" of computers and their users. The conglomerate information and resources of the Internet and other networked communication services.

DARPA   See **Defense Advanced Research Projects Agency.**

Database   Any collection of data or interrelated files that can be accessed in a variety of ways.

Decode   To convert an encoded file back to its original form. See also **Encode.**

Dedicated line   A single-purpose connection providing uninterrupted service, as with cable television or a leased telephone line.

Defense Advanced Research Projects Agency (DARPA) An agency of the U.S. Department of Defense responsible for the development of new military technology. DARPA (formerly known as ARPA) was responsible for the funding and development of the Internet.

DELPHI   A major on-line service, the first to provide full Internet access.

Demo   An abridged or otherwise limited version of a software program for demonstration or trial purposes.

Dialup account   A form of Internet access providing a temporary, as opposed to dedicated, telephone connection.

Digital   Generally, using numbers or other discrete units–as with a digital, as opposed to analog, watch. The term is synonymous with any binary coded system or device, hence essentially synonymous with *computer*.

Directory   An index of the location of files, as on a hard drive of a computer. Directories create the illusion of file drawers, even though the files may be physically dispersed.

Discussion Group   A forum in which subscribers communicate by exchanging group E-mail messages.

Domain   A portion of the hierarchical system used for identifying Internet addresses. Key domains include: .COM (commercial), .EDU (educational), .NET (network operations), .GOV (government), and .MIL (military).

Domain Name System (DNS)   The system for translating alphabetic computer addresses into numerical addresses.

DOS (Disk Operating System)   Generally, any computer operating system. More specifically, the operating system used in IBM-compatible PCs (for example, PC-DOS, MS-DOS, or DR-DOS).

DOS prompt   A set of characters displayed on screen to indicate that DOS is ready to accept a command from the user. The default DOS prompt is C:\>.

Download   To receive information or files from a remote computer.

E-mail   Electronic mail.

Electronic texts   Texts encoded for electronic storage or transmission.

Emoticon   A symbol used to indicate emotion or the equivalent of a voice inflection in an E-mail message. See also **Smiley.**

Encode   To convert a file from one format to another, as from binary to ASCII for E-mail transmission.

Encryption   The coding of data for purposes of secrecy and/or security.

Ethernet   A form of local area network offering communication at 2–10 megabits per second. See also **Local area network.**

Extension   An abbreviation (usually three-digit) added to file names to indicate the file format.

FAQ   See **Frequently asked question.**

FedWorld   The federally funded bulletin board providing access to many U.S. government agency bulletin boards.

FidoNet   A hobbyist network primarily for personal E-mail messages and group postings. Accessible from many bulletin boards.

File   Stored computer data representing text, numeric, sound, or graphic images.

File transfer protocol (FTP)   A program for transferring files from one computer (a host) to another (a client), especially for retrieving files from public archives. See also **Anonymous FTP.**

Flame   A strong statement, usually of an inflammatory and personal nature, in an electronic mail message.

Floppy disk   A portable plastic disk for storing computer files as magnetic impulses.

Freenet   A community-based bulletin board system providing free local information and/or Internet access. Often established through public libraries and/or as part of the National Public Telecomputing Network (NPTN).

Freeware   Computer programs made available to the public with no cost or copyright restriction.

Frequently asked question (FAQ)   A common name for files compiling answers to common questions, hence providing introductory information on a topic. Often appearing in newsgroups.

FTP   See **File transfer protocol.**

Gateway   A device, program, or site providing access to a network, generally between otherwise incompatible formats or protocols.

Geek-talk   The vernacular of the Internet. Nerd-speak.

GEnie (General Electric Network for Information Exchange)   An on-line service.

Gigabyte   One billion bytes.

Gopher   A hierarchical menu program for accessing information across the Internet.

Gopherspace   That part of the Internet accessible by Gopher, that is, on Gopher servers and listed in Gopher menus.

Graphic interface   A computer interface that displays graphic elements and icons rather than only lines of simple text. A computer interface negotiated with a mouse as well as with cursor keys.

Handshake   The procedure by which communications programs recognize the speed and protocol of messages.

Hardware   Physical components of a computer, such as keyboards, monitors, and modems, as opposed to software.

Home page   An initial menu page of a World Wide Web site, written in Hypertext Markup Language (HTML).

Host   A computer that allows other computers to communicate with it.

HTML   See **Hypertext Markup Language.**

Hypertext Markup Language (HTML)   The system of embedding retrieval commands and associated addresses within a text; used for documents on the World Wide Web.

Hypertext Transfer Protocol   The program controlling the transmission of documents and other files over the World Wide Web.

Hytelnet   A menu-driven version of telnet. A menu of telnet sites.

Icon   A graphical representation or symbol representing a file, program, or command on graphic-interface programs.

Interface   The connection between two devices. More particularly, the nature of the display screen used for communication between user and computer.

Internet   The worldwide "network of networks" connected to each other using the Internet protocol and other similar protocols. The Internet provides file transfer, remote login, electronic mail, and other services.

Internet Hunt (The)   A monthly contest offering a set of questions to be answered utilizing resources of the Internet.

Internet Protocol (IP)   A protocol involving packets of data traversing multiple networks. The protocol on which the Internet is based.

Internet Service Provider   A national or local company providing access to the Internet.

Internet Society (ISOC)   A nonprofit, professional membership organization that sets Internet policy and promotes its use through forums and the collaboration of members.

IP   See **Internet Protocol.**

IP address   The 32-bit address, defined by the Internet Protocol and represented in dotted decimal notation, cf. 171.292.292.23, assigned to a computer on a TCP/IP network.

ISDN (Integrated Services Digital Network) A digital telephone line operating at 64,000 bits per second, and up to 128,000 bps with special protocols.

ISOC See **Internet Society.**

Jughead (Jonzy's Universal Gopher Hierarchy Excavation and Display) A variant of Veronica that searches directories on a select number of gophers.

Kb (kilobits) 1,024 bits of information.

KB (kilobytes) 1,024 bytes of information.

Key-word search program A program for searching a database or set of files for a specific term or terms.

LAN See **Local area network.**

Listserv One of a number of listserver programs.

Listserver An automated mailing list distribution program providing the basis of many mailing list subscription or discussion groups.

Local area network (LAN) A computer network limited to an individual building, series of offices, or other small area.

Logoff To relinquish access to a computer network.

Logon To gain access to a remote computer or computer network.

Lurking Just listening. Passive examination of information, generally out of curiosity or as a means of learning standard behaviors prior to participating on a newsgroup or chat program. Lurking has no adverse connotations.

Mailing list A system of forwarding messages to groups of people via E-mail.

Megabit (Mb) One million bits.

Megabyte (MB) One million bytes.

Metasearch program A program offering a common interface for a variety of search programs.

Microsoft Windows A graphic-interface operating system from Microsoft Corporation for IBM-compatible computers.

Modem (*Mo***dulate/***Dem***odulate)** A device that enables computers to transmit and receive information over telephone lines by converting between digital and analog signals.

Mosaic The initial World Wide Web browser program.

MUD See **Multi-User Dungeon.**

Multimedia Integrating text, sound, and graphics.

Multisearch program A program offering simultaneous searches of a number of search programs.

Multi-User Dungeon (MUD) Adventure and role-playing games or simulations, modeled after Dungeons and Dragons.

National Science Foundation (NSF) A U.S. government agency devoted to promoting the advancement of scientific research and understanding.

Netiquette Proper social behavior on a network.

Netscape A leading World Wide Web browser program.

Network A communication system consisting of two or more computers or other devices.

Network Information Centers (NICs) Organizations providing documentation, guidance, advice, and assistance for a specific network.

NSFnet A high-speed backbone network sponsored by the National Science Foundation.

Ntalk New talk, a new form of talk program. See also **Talk.**

On Ramp See **Gateway.**

On-line fee A transmission charge based on connection time.

On-line service A centralized computer network offering subscribers a variety of services including E-mail, file transfers, chat groups, and business, entertainment, and educational materials. Any service accessed by telephone.

Operating system The primary program of a computer, cf. MD-DOS, Windows, Macintosh System 7. The operating system determines the basic commands and the appearance of the screen.

Packet A bundle of data sent across a network (usually less than 1,500 bytes).

Packet switching A communications paradigm in which packets of information are individually routed between hosts with no previously established communication path.

Parallel search program A program offering simultaneous searches by a number of search programs.

Password A word or code used to identify an authorized user.

Point and click The process for entering commands in a graphics-interface operating system using a mouse or similar device.

Point-to-Point Protocol (PPP) A method for using the Internet

TCP/IP protocol over telephone lines, hence for providing direct Internet access via modem. The replacement for **SLIP.**

Prodigy One of the top three on-line services.

Prompt A message or signal in a computer program requesting action by the user. See also **DOS prompt.**

Protocol A formal description of operating rules.

Search program Any program providing direct examination of a database.

Serial Line IP (SLIP) A program for using the Internet TCP/IP protocol over telephone lines, hence for providing Internet access via modem. SLIP is being superseded by Point-to-Point Protocol.

Server A host computer serving a special function or offering resources for client computers, whether as a storage device in a local area network or as a Gopher site on the Internet.

Shareware Commercial software available initially free on a trial basis.

Shell account A form of Internet access utilizing the programs and access of the Internet service provider. Indirect access to the Internet.

SLIP See **Serial Line IP.**

Smiley An icon used to convey emotion or innuendo in texts, e.g., **:-)** (glad), **:-[** (disappointment).

Snail mail A pejorative term referring to the U.S. postal service.

Software Computer programs, as opposed to hardware. See also **Hardware.**

Spamming Deluging someone with unwanted messages as punishment for inappropriate use of an on-line service or the Internet.

Spreadsheet A computer program simulating the columns of a numerical worksheet, as for budgets.

Surfing Random or otherwise seemingly undirected browsing, as of the World Wide Web.

System Operator (Sysop) The administrator of a bulletin board service.

System 7 A Macintosh operating system.

T1 An intermediate-level network cable carrying a digital signal at 1.544 megabits per second.

T3 A top-level or backbone network cable carrying a digital signal at 44.746 megabits per second.

Talk A program in which two users exchange on-screen messages.

TCP/IP–Transmission Control Protocol/Internet Protocol The packet-switching communications protocol on which Internet communication is based.

Telecommunication The sending and receiving of messages over long distances.

Telnet An Internet program for accessing remote computers.

Text interface A screen display limited to lines of keyboard characters.

Uniform resource locator (URL) A format for indicating the protocol and address for accessing information on the Internet; a name identifying documents and services on the Internet.

Unix A popular operating system important in the development of the Internet.

Upload To send files to a remote computer.

URL See **Uniform resource locator.**

Usenet A network and program for reading and posting messages on public newsgroups; accessible in whole or in part via the Internet or many on-line services.

User An individual who interacts with a computer.

User interface The combination of menus, screen design, keyboard commands, and language that together determine how a user interacts with a computer.

User-friendly A term that implies a system or program that is easy to learn and use.

Userid A user's identification code name.

Username See **Userid.**

Vaporware Computer programs that have been announced but not as yet released; hence programs that claim to be extraordinarily powerful and error free.

Veronica (Very Easy Rodent-Oriented Net-Wide Index of Computerized Archives) A program developed at the University of Nevada at Reno in late 1992 for searching Gopher menus.

Virus A rogue software program that attaches itself to other programs and is designed to erase files or otherwise disrupt the proper functioning of computers.

WAIS See **Wide Area Information Server.**

WAN See **Wide area network.**

Wide Area Information Server (WAIS) A program for searching collections of documents for specific terms.

Wide area network A computer network extending over a wide area. See also **Local area network.**

Word processor A computer program that replaces all the operations normally associated with a typewriter.

World Wide Web (WWW) A hypertext-based system for finding and accessing Internet resources.

WYSIWYG (What You See Is What You Get) A format for word processor programs in which the onscreen representation is identical to subsequent printer output.